HALF MY SIZE
HOW I ATE TO LOSE 150LBS!

HALF MY SIZE

HOW I ATE TO LOSE 150LBS!

CAROLINE JHINGORY

Half My Size: How I Ate to Lose 150lbs!

Crittenden Publishing

ISBN: 978-0-9886981-0-9

Author Website: CarolineJhingory.com

"After" Author Photography: PrincepsStudio.com
"Food Addict" Photography: Trasher Photography
Cover Design and Interior Layout: AuthorSupport.com

To give you a taste of what is to come, here are the 10 "Caroline's Commandments" on healthy eating that I offer in the coming chapters. Reflecting the parallels between food and drug addiction, these were inspired by Notorious B.I.G.'s 10 crack commandments.

1. Don't make the term "food addiction" your crutch.
2. It takes a village to lose weight.
3. Never begin a diet that you can't do for the rest of your life.
4. Just because something is "healthy," "organic," or "natural" does not mean it will help you lose weight.
5. Heroin, crack, and carbohydrates are first cousins.
6. Lean protein and non-starchy vegetables: Thou shalt have no other foods but me.
7. Sugar is the crack, not cocaine, of the food world.
8. Black girls shouldn't eat carbs.
9. Exercise! The drug everyone can afford!
10. Happy 30th birthday! It is also your metabolism's retirement party!

TABLE OF CONTENTS

TABLE OF CONTENTS *(continued)*

TABLE OF CONTENTS *(continued)*

PREFACE

I AM NOT a doctor, a nutritionist, a personal trainer, or a hypnotherapist. But I am a person who lost 150 pounds and has managed to keep it off for more than a decade. I am Caroline Jhingory. And like most of you, I am a person who loves to eat. This is my story of how a recovering food addict lost the weight, kept it off, and can hopefully provide you with a plan to do the same.

ACKNOWLEDGEMENTS

FIRST, I WOULD like to thank my mother, Marsha, for her invaluable support throughout my life. My determination and ability to lose weight and to keep it off for 10 years has led some people to call me amazing or incredible, but I am simply my mother's daughter. Every bit of my spirit and will comes from her. Mommy, thank you for being there when I failed, when I almost made it, and when I succeeded. You have been my constant cheerleader, and you are the truest personification of unconditional love. My love for you is beyond measure.

I also thank various individuals for their support over the years. At the top of this list is my stepfather, Roscoe. Thank you for loving me and my mom so much and for instilling in me an unwavering love for the Washington Redskins. My father, Joseph, for constantly telling me to "write a book, nah man," and my entire Lancaster, Ridley, Mootoo, Jhingory, and Ellis family. Alma Morena Davenport, my best friend for the last 16 years, you haven't been *like* a sister, you *are* my sister. Charisse and Harvey Nunes and Mirian Torain, I appreciate you all for being my second family. Charisse, a huge hug for also connecting me with D'Amari Jackson. I am extremely grateful to all of the professors and teachers I have had throughout my life. My college professors, Dr. Robert Hayden, Dr. Sheila Peters, Dr. Adam Meyer, and Professor Cindi Lanza, extracted thoughts and ideas from my brain that I didn't even know were there; thank you, too, for your support beyond the classroom. Because of the amazing faculty and staff at the Duke Ellington School of the Arts, I consider my days as a student there the best time of my life. Peggy Cooper Cafritz, Mike Malone, Lew Berry, Carolyn Jones–Howard, Joan Van Der Mortel, David Aaronson, Cullen Swinson, John Payne, and Treva Lindsey, thank you all for providing children in the District of Columbia with an outlet for the creative arts.

At my graduation from the Duke Ellington School of the Arts, actress Phylicia Rashad said, "Young people, don't make it your goal in life to be successful. Make it your goal to serve humanity." I hope that through this manual, I am doing just that.

DISCLAIMER

THIS MANUAL CANNOT give you medical advice or diagnosis. Nothing contained in this manual should be construed as such medical advice or diagnosis. The information in this manual should not be interpreted as a substitute for physician consultation, evaluation, or treatment. You are urged and advised to seek the advice of a physician before beginning any weight loss effort or regimen and to never disregard professional medical advice or to delay seeking medical treatment because of something you have read in this manual. The information in this manual is intended for use only by healthy adult individuals. It is not intended for use by minors, pregnant women, or individuals with any type of health condition. Such individuals are specifically warned to seek professional medical advice prior to initiating any form of weight loss effort or regimen.

INTRODUCTION

THE 300-POUND SCHOOLGIRL

From elementary to high school I was the fat and ugly big black girl, the "hey, hey, Fat Albert" girl, the Grimace girl, the Mack truck girl—the one everyone asked, "Goddamn girl, why don't you lose some weight?" I weighed 120 pounds in the third grade and by high school had ballooned to 300 pounds. Not only was I overweight, I had dark brown skin, and the world saw this as a second reason to strike. Whenever someone described me or wanted to make a joke, somehow my weight and dark skin tone were always combined. "You know Caroline, that fat dark-skinned girl," or "She looks like a giant black jelly bean!" To get people to like me, I tried to be the "funny girl." Also, I often acted out to get sent home from school, and I went as far as telling my parents that I had scarlet fever or smallpox so that I wouldn't have to attend school at all.

Insults and negative comments about my weight weren't restricted to kids at school. Both kids and adults in my neighborhood—and even family—couldn't help commenting on my weight. When I was 10 years old, comments such as "If you don't lose weight, how do you expect to find a husband?" didn't sound like concern: they just hurt. My preferred method of coping became multiple microwaveable pizzas, chicken nuggets, entire packs of deli meat, and Snickers bars hidden under my bed.

In elementary school I was a food hustler, trading stickers and glow-in-the-dark pencils for Hostess cupcakes, Lunchables, and Cheez Whiz and crackers. After school, I pretended I had forgotten my keys just to go visit my retired 70-year-old neighbor who, no matter what time of the year it was, had Thanksgiving-like food available. She fed me ham, macaroni and cheese, biscuits, and homemade pound cake. I did not have money or a job, but I made every effort to get the food I wanted. By middle school I had become an even more seasoned hustler, stealing money from the giant soda bottle piggy bank where my stepfather had emptied his loose change and dollars every day for years. It was enough money to support my habit of Chinese takeout, candy, multiple Huggies juices, and Funyuns from the convenience store.

EATING MY WAY THROUGH LONELINESS

Why was I so hungry? I certainly did not recognize it then, but now I wonder if I was filling the void of my biological father's absence. When I was a young child, my father and I had been BFFs. I was his first daughter, and he even named me after his mother, Caroline, who had died in his native Guyana while my mother was pregnant with me. Like many West Indian men, my dad was always into fixing stuff: things around the house, cars, or even things that didn't need fixing. My mom told me that when I was a baby, she would get up at 2 a.m. to check on me, and she'd find me in my walker wearing nothing but a diaper and sucking on a curry chicken bone while watching my father work. If she tried to take me back to bed, I'd holler and scream, and my dad in his Guyanese accent would say, "Leave she, leave she." I still have memories of fishing with my father, catching giant catfish and rainbow trout or making salt fish and bake with him on Saturday mornings and listening to him sing a Guyanese song about a woman named Lou-Lou. During my parents' separation and then divorce, my father disappeared from my life—even though he lived just 30 minutes away. Not only did I lose my daddy, but I also lost my first best friend. To this day I have no clear understanding of why, nor has he provided me with any answers.

After my father vanished from my life, I got bigger and bigger and the teasing became more cruel. There was one place, though, where I felt normal—with my teenage cousins, Tameka and Sabrina. They styled my hair so that together we looked like J.J. Fad, let me play with their makeup, and made me a background dancer in their remakes of Salt-n-Pepa videos. The three of us almost broke our necks when we tried to do the chair routines from Janet Jackson's "I Miss You Much" video. They came to get me almost every weekend for sleepovers at one of their houses. Everywhere they went, I went too: to the hairdresser, the mall, to meet up with their boyfriends at the park (if I promised not to tell). At the mall teenage boys—and some grown men—would ooh and ahh at how gorgeous they were.

Even though the boys weren't oohing and aahing at me, people always said they could tell Tameka and I were cousins because of our very thick eyebrows. And Sabrina and I had the same deep dark brown skin and Colgate smiles, although she never had braces. I looked a little like each of them, and I loved being with my cousins in public because when people told them how beautiful they were, it made me feel beautiful too. They were also my bulletproof jackets against the world's fat jokes. My cousins would quickly check anyone that attempted to insult their "lil' cuzzin," and when I was with them, I was in a temporary cocoon.

On August 11, 1994, the summer before high school, my stepfather woke up my brother and me and brought us into his and my mom's bedroom. I actually thought one of us was in trouble for not washing the dishes. My cousins had been killed in a violent car accident. The brakes had failed in the beat-up car they had worked to buy themselves. The car had crashed into a retaining wall just blocks from the U.S. Capitol, and Tameka's body was flung through the windshield. An old car battery in the back seat rocketed forward and crushed Sabrina's skull.

A few months after my cousins died, I was wearing plus size 26 jeans and had begun to act out in school. I talked back to my teachers and deliberately tried to piss them off. I was often suspended and eventually had to transfer schools. That car crash took away my cousins and my "security blanket," and in my life things went from bad to worse. I felt alone and hollow, and all I wanted to do was fill the painful void with food. Food helped me escape my grief and my anger about my cousins' violent and gruesome death. I began to question everything I'd been taught to believe about God in my Catholic school religion classes. I felt that God must hate me, so I began to hate myself. And these feelings were intensified by the nonstop teasing and fat jokes.

Then and now people often ask, "Where were your parents when you were going through this?" My mother and stepfather were dedicated parents and tried everything to help me lose weight. They enrolled me in dance and exercise classes at our church; entered me in a pediatric medical weight-loss program with counseling at Children's National Medical Center in my hometown of Washington, D.C.; and stocked our cabinets with healthy food suggested by doctors. I resisted. My food hustler spirit was alive and well. In the middle of the night when everyone was sleeping, I used to get up and binge on leftovers from dinner. Not even a well-balanced, home-cooked meal is healthy when you eat multiple portions of it.

Food for me was what alcohol, cigarettes, drugs, and sex are for other addicts: a way to escape and suppress pain. I couldn't think rationally—to see that my overeating was the cause of my classmates' teasing and my family's disappointment. I didn't see and didn't care, and my sole objective was to hide in food, no matter how detrimental it was to my health. I gorged on food to suppress the pain, and, like every other addict, my addiction made it feel like Christmas morning and fireworks combined when I was using but like crap once the high faded.

THE FINAL STRAW

There was no life-changing incident that was my aha moment. Instead, one day when I was home from college I just said to myself, "I have had enough!" *Enough* of wearing girdles to fit into outfits, *enough* of being the girl that guys never notice. Being obese had caused me to miss simple but important pleasures in life. I had not worn a bathing suit since I was 9 years old, I had never been able to ride a roller coaster because the safety bar did not fit over my stomach, I had never been to a school dance and had missed my prom, and I had never had a boyfriend.

My weight loss journey was one of trial and error—and more error than trial. I tried becoming a vegetarian, drinking only Slim-Fast, and getting B12 injections in my butt cheek once a week. I even tried Walmart-brand weight loss pills that other girls in my dorm were using. Sure, I lost a little weight here and there, but I also felt tired and grumpy (*likely because I was hungry* and dehydrated). The weight always came back.

HOW I LOST THE WEIGHT

I finally found help from my family doctor, who was a mix of Fred Samford and Cliff Huxtable. His first bit of nutrition advice was, "Just don't eat anything white." He explained that this meant eliminating my intake of foods made with flour, sugar, dairy, rice, and starchy vegetables like potatoes and corn; which are yellow, but you get the point. For exercise he told me to walk halfway home from the summer internship I had at the time before catching the bus. Each day I walked as much as I could until I finally made it all the way home without the bus. The combination of that hilly walk home in the D.C. summer heat and eliminating white foods must have scared my body straight. Within the first month I bought a belt for the first time in my life because my clothes had gotten so loose. Over time my body started to crave more of a challenge, so I joined a gym and worked with a personal trainer for two months (because it was all I could afford) to get guidance on how to use various machines in the gym. Once I got the hang of things, I began using new machines like the elliptical trainer and increasing how long and how often I exercised (45 to 60 minutes, six days a week) and added resistance training every other day. In addition to exercise, I did my best to cook and eat my own food the majority of the time. It took me a year to lose the weight and another year to learn how to keep it off. And as I've gotten older and my metabolism has slowed down, I've had to add tweaks to both how I eat and how I exercise. This method of healthy eating evolved from a temporary solution into a permanent lifestyle.

I finally accepted there are no shortcuts or secrets to weight loss. My first piece of advice is for you to do the same.

CHAPTER 1
FIGHTING THE ADDICTION

I LOVE FOOD. When someone surprises me with a red velvet cupcake, I do the same crackhead shuffle dance that Samuel L. Jackson did in the movie *Jungle Fever*. During Thanksgiving and Christmas I sing and perform "Food Glorious Food" in my parents' kitchen when my stepsister lets me lick the leftover sweet potato pie filling from the mixing bowl. As a teenager I used my allowance money to buy and eat 12-inch steak-and-cheese subs and multiple packages of Oreos alone in the basement. It felt soooo good while I was doing it, but I always felt bad about myself afterward. I still have the obsession with food that caused me to weigh over 300 pounds in middle school. I consider myself a food addict in the present tense. My own challenges with overeating and my career experience as a social worker have taught me that addictions are never cured: *Once an addict, always an addict.* The hunger—for food or whatever you're addicted to—never goes away. Instead, we just learn to better manage our addictions. We also learn to recognize ourselves first as people who are not defined by their addictions. I am not the food addict Caroline, but I am Caroline an individual who continues her recovery from food addiction.

Emotional eating is the gateway drug to food addiction. Emotional eating is not just about eating when you are sad or depressed: It is eating for reasons other than actually being physically hungry. Prior to beginning my journey I used to eat family-size bags of potato chips because I was bored. When I was happy I would want a treat like a trip to the Cheesecake Factory. And when I actually did feel sad or depressed, I became a human vacuum, wanting everything from ice cream to entire tubs of raw chocolate chip cookie dough. Food was always convenient and accessible. I wanted more, and it provided me with the instant gratification to match whatever emotion I was feeling at the time. We all eat for emotional reasons sometimes. But it becomes a problem when we overeat so often that it causes us to gain 100 pounds or more and leads to health ailments such as heart disease and diabetes. The first step in overcoming emotional eating or food addiction is recognizing it.

Here are some possible signs of food addiction—many that I was guilty of before beginning my weight loss journey:

You continue to eat when you're already full.

- Despite telling yourself you will have only one serving or one slice of something, you end up having multiple servings, eating the entire pie . . . or taking the entire pie home and waking up at 2 a.m. to eat the rest.
- You steal other people's food.
- You have pulled food from a garbage can and eaten it.
- You eat to the point of feeling ill or as if you have to vomit. And despite feeling ill or as if you have to vomit, you continue to eat.
- You go out of your way to get a particular food if it's not available.
- You eat food as if you were a prison inmate: rapidly and guarding the food as if someone will steal it.
- Instead of working or spending time with

family and friends, you make up excuses to stay at home and eat.

- You have problems focusing at school or work because of thoughts about food.
- You store food in your purse, your car, your desk at work, your nightstand—everywhere. Also, you keep a food trash bag in your car.
- You drive to deserted locations such as empty parking lots to eat multiple fast food value meals that you just bought at the drive-thru.
- You avoid professional or social situations where certain foods are available because of fear of overeating.
- You would rather have food than sex.
- You are aroused, not jokingly, by food as if it were sex.

FINDING HELP FOR FOOD ADDICTION

Treating food addiction requires a stronger prescription than taking a walk or phoning a friend when you feel the urge to overdose on pasta and brownies. There are programs such as Food Addicts in Recovery Anonymous and Food Addicts Anonymous that use principles that are similar to those of the 12-step programs that have helped many recover from addictions to alcohol, sex, drugs, and gambling. Also, seek out a nutritionist, psychologist, or doctor who specializes in the treatment of food addiction and may be able to help you break your compulsive eating habits. In addition to possibly treating your food addiction, these professionals can help with identifying and resolving the full gambit of issues that may be adversely affecting your life. Consider my manual as only one tool of many that you will need to reach your weight loss goals. I encourage anyone who considers herself an emotional eater or a food addict to see a licensed psychotherapist or join a support group led by one. Although your religious leader, life coach, mother, and best friend can provide helpful support, they do not qualify as a psychotherapist—unless that person has an actual license. Therapy is extremely important to successful weight loss. You must not only understand but also resolve the issues that cause you to look to food for comfort because weight loss alone does nothing to cause stress loss, problem loss, people-in-your-life-working-your-last-nerve loss. However, therapy combined with exercise and the approach to healthy eating outlined in this manual may help you shed more than a few pounds. Therapy isn't just "healing your emotional wounds" or other clichés you hear on television. Therapy teaches you to use emotional wounds as fuel and motivation to get your life in order. To find a qualified psychotherapist, check with your insurance company, speak with your primary care physician or ob/gyn, or ask trusted friends and family members for referrals.

CAROLINE'S COMMANDMENT #1

Don't make the term "food addiction" your crutch.

Food addiction is real, but many people don't meet the clinical definition of "food addiction." Many Americans want what they want, when they want it, and lots of it. Over the years, I have had several adult men and women ask me, "How can I eat whatever I want and still lose weight?" This has often made me say that delusion would be a better diagnosis than food addiction. Just as with everything else in life, if you want something badly enough, you must be patient and disciplined, and willing to put in 100 percent to get what you want. I've watched people sacrifice and go above and beyond for cars, homes, boyfriends—yet be unwilling to put in the same effort to lose weight and possibly save their lives. Use the discipline and sacrifice you applied to other situations in your life, and put that towards resisting the craving for Lays when you are at the supermarket or the urge to gorge on pasta because you felt that you deserved to treat yourself. Don't look to food to treat yourself. Instead focus on treating yourself to a healthier body and longer life

LOSE THE WEIGHT, DON'T WAIT TO LOSE!

I don't believe weight loss should be slow and gradual. The one place I will say I am like most Americans is that I wanted the instant gratification of seeing week-to-week weight loss results, and the methods I have outlined in this manual did just that for me. I believe that when individuals don't see week-to-week results they are more likely to give up and fall back on poor eating habits. Still, my method is not easy, nor do I offer any "tricks" to weight loss. Really, the words "simple," "easy," and "tricks" have no place in the weight loss world. You will need to make a complete transformation of how you are eating. You may miss certain foods, but your stomach will never grumble, and you will never have an I'm-hungry-as-hell headache like you did with other diets. **I don't have all the answers, but I am confident that some of the information provided here can help you in your weight loss journey.** Just as in alcohol or drug abuse support groups, people are most successful when sponsored by an individual who has overcome similar obstacles. *Hello, my name is Caroline, and I am former food addict, emotional eater, and a survivor of acute depression and low self-esteem who has spent 20 years of my life as morbidly obese and lost 150 pounds and maintained the weight loss for a decade.* So perhaps we share similar obstacles, and through this manual I can be your virtual sponsor in helping you overcome your weight and emotional issues. Consider me the weight loss whisperer!

WHY ARE WE SO FAT?

I am tired of hearing that Americans are fat because they sit at home watching too much reality television and eat too much junk food. I am also sick of hearing that black women don't exercise because they are worried about their hair.

But let's call it like it is. There *is* some truth to both of these statements.

However, there are a good number of Americans—including black women—who exercise five or more days a week and at least *think* they are eating healthy yet still can't lose weight. One of the key reasons for this is that the current health information provided by TV doctors, morning talk show nutritionists, health magazines, and their websites or blogs leads people to believe that:

1. Detoxes, cleansing, and fasting are healthy weight loss methods.
2. Foods made with dairy products and wheat are a necessary part of daily diet.
3. Reducing meat consumption is needed for weight loss.
4. Sugar can be consumed in moderation and that "*healthy sugars*" exist.

Instead, this misinformation causes people to stay at the same weight or even gain weight. Then they go right back to the same unreliable source for more misguided information. It's not unlike the relationship between drug dealer and junkie where the goal is to keep you coming back again and again. You may ask, "If this health information is inaccurate, then why do they put it out there?" The food companies that make products containing wheat, dairy, and sugar heavily finance the platforms used to disseminate this misinformation. You also have to question who is funding these allegedly objective research studies that encourage us to eat all these foods.

I know that these weight loss methods do not work from using my own body as a litmus test for what it truly takes to lose 150 pounds and keep the weight off for a decade. The advice in this manual is not a digest of research studies, a discussion of realistic versus unrealistic weight loss, or a list of health facts. I present what has worked and continues to work for me in losing weight and keeping it off. The healthy eating philosophies I share go against everything you learned about the food pyramid in kindergarten—but it has worked for me. As a result of my methods, to date I have no known health ailments or limitations. In my Olivia-from-*The-Cosby-Show* voice, "*I'm still alive!*" Eating this way and losing weight actually improved my overall health from when I weighed over 300 pounds. The pre-diabetic dark blotches on my skin have disappeared, my back and joint problems are gone, and whenever a nurse takes my blood pressure,

I'm always told, "*Wow, that's really good.*" I chose to focus on healthy eating in this manual because experience has taught me that weight loss is 85 percent what you eat and 15 percent exercise. Still, weight loss is more comprehensive than just eating healthy and getting off your butt to go to the gym. To be successful, you need to be disciplined, understand your body's chemistry, and keep your mental health in check, so I discuss these as well.

CAROLINE'S COMMANDMENT #2

It takes a village to lose weight..

It takes a village to raise a child, and it also takes a village to successfully lose weight. In addition to professional help (if that's a path you decide to take), you will also need a positive support system of faith, family, and friends. These individuals will directly and indirectly act as your cheerleaders and also help to hold you accountable in meeting your weight loss goals.

FINDING YOUR VILLAGE

Below, I provide specific examples of the people you need and don't need during your weight loss journey.

PEOPLE YOU NEED

- Folks willing to be your daily exercise partner and call or text you to remind you of workouts.
- Individuals who always forward you emails for things like discounted gym memberships, healthy cooking classes, or coupons on fitness clothes.
- A friend who reminds you, "*Girl, it ain't worth it*," when you see a waiter go by with a slice of cheesecake in a restaurant.
- A significant other who, instead of picking up takeout from a greasy spoon joint on the way home, cooks you a healthy meal (and feeds it to you), brings you flowers, and who constantly lets you know, "***Damn baby, you look good***!" throughout your weight loss journey.
- Relatives who make sure there are healthy options readily available for you at family events where potato salad and fried chicken have already RSVP'd.

I promise you molding your support system to be like this will not come easy.

PEOPLE YOU DON'T NEED

- Friends who know you are trying to lose weight, yet still constantly invite you out for cupcakes or to happy hours with sugary alcoholic drinks and half-off appetizers of mini-burgers, onion rings, and quesadillas.
- "Friends" whose compliments are mixed with insults, such as "*You look good, but girl, you know you ain't gonna lose no weight.*"
- Anyone who laughs at how you look in your exercise clothes.
- Individuals who dance and wave around food in your face that you are not supposed to have.
- A significant other that gives you an ultimatum to lose weight and threatens to leave you.
- Morbidly obese aunts, grandmothers, and other relatives who say you are already "too skinny" when a physician has said that you are 50 pounds or more overweight.

Okay, so you may not be able to give everyone the deuces, especially family members. Still, weight loss is a process of sacrifice and selfishness. Weight loss is a lifestyle change, which also means changing some of the people in your life—*especially the ones that cause you to emotionally eat*—and changing the activities you do with the people who stay in your life. During your weight loss journey, you will have to retrain people how to treat and speak to you. Think of everyone in your life like an elevator: Either they can bring you up or down. If a person constantly takes you to a level that is beneath you, you may have to give them the pink slip from your life, no matter who they are.

CAROLINE'S COMMANDMENT #3

Never begin a diet that you can't do for the rest of your life.

When I started my weight loss journey, my doctor gave me an important suggestion besides "Don't eat anything white." I will always remember this tip: "Never, ever begin a diet that you can't do for the rest of your life." Why? Because, if you can't do the diet for the rest of your life, then you won't do it for the rest of your life. You will only end up with a temporary weight loss reward, and all of the weight you lose will return with friends.

HABITS FOR LIFE

Any style of eating that prohibits chewable foods will cause you to feel tired, bitchy and eventually binge and eat everything in sight, especially if you are an emotional eater. Also, food deprivation diets such as the Master Cleanse, liquid diets, and pill poppin' could possibly cause more health problems and leave you more frustrated and depressed than when you initially started. People have explained to me that they do fasts or detoxes to allegedly "jumpstart" their weight loss. Beginning a weight loss plan does not require a fast. A better start would be jumping on a treadmill and going fast.

Our bodies need no extra cleansing. In a healthy body, the liver and kidneys are capable of eliminating toxins on their own. Using detox kits and cayenne pepper/lemon juice/maple syrup concoctions is like adding extra Clorox to a load of laundry that you're washing with a detergent with bleach. The body does not ever need a "food break"—just as a car never needs a gas break.

In the long run starving your body of food makes you fatter. Even worse, not getting enough nutrients from real food causes your body to eat into muscle for energy, which slows down your metabolism. It then becomes harder to burn calories because your body conserves what little energy it gets. Your body holds on to existing fat like a hostage because it doesn't know when you will feed it again!

Most celebrities do detoxes and cleanses as a quick slim down for upcoming movie roles or award shows, not for health. If a personal trainer or nutritionist tries to sell you "cleansing–detox products," run like hell. They know that the products are useless, but, like you and me, they have bills to pay and know that people would even buy anthrax if someone told them it produced weight loss. Detoxes are only needed for the big stuff: coke, heroin, prescription drugs, and alcohol—not weight loss.

CHAPTER 2

MY PRINCIPLES ON HEALTHY EATING

CAROLINE'S COMMANDMENT #4

Just because something is "healthy," "organic," or "natural" does not mean it will help you lose weight.

BEFORE YOU BEGIN reading my principles to healthy eating, please keep in mind that just because a food is nutritious or labeled natural or organic does not mean it will help you lose weight.

FOODS LABELED "ORGANIC," "NATURAL," OR "HEALTHY"

The Food and Drug Administration gives food companies extreme latitude in using words like "healthy" and "natural." There are almost no regulations. Remember when Wendy's was allowed to say that their French fries deep-fried in oil with sea salt were natural and healthy? Be suspicious of these labels. In most cases, especially if it's packaged in a box or in plastic, they're not healthy or natural. They can have high carbohydrate content or be filled with additives. Foods that are truly natural or healthy, such as lean meat and fresh non-starchy vegetables, usually require refrigeration and don't sit on unrefrigerated shelves of the grocery store.

While there are still some refrigerated foods that market themselves as healthy, organic or natural, they still can stall weight loss. For example, both yogurt and granola often carry these labels. Even those yogurts without added high-fructose corn syrup contain lactose, which is a sugar, and sugar, no matter what its form, stalls weight loss. Likewise, granola may be loaded with fiber but is also mostly sugar and fat. This also goes for trendy health foods like turkey bacon and almond milk. Both are processed foods that are often made with sugar and some other form of carbohydrate. Turkey and almonds in their natural state must go through a hell of a *process*—which in some cases includes adding hard-to-pronounce food additives, sugar, and food colorings—to make them into something they originally were not. Stick to eating foods that are in the natural state as much as possible. The information in this section will help you read between the lines when it comes to alleged "healthy foods" and carbohydrates overall. Lastly, please remember that I am not the doctor or nutritionist Caroline, just Caroline. Some of my food science philosophies may not be exact, but they enabled me to lose the exact amount of weight I wanted to lose . . . and once again, "I'm still alive!"

Now, let's get to it. Here are my principles to healthy eating in a nutshell:

- Heroin, crack, and carbohydrates are first cousins.
- Lean protein and non-starchy vegetables: Thou shalt have no other foods but me.
- Sugar is the crack, not cocaine, of the food world.
- Black girls shouldn't eat carbs.

CAROLINE'S COMMANDMENT #5

Heroin, crack, and carbohydrates are cousins.

INSULIN AND WHY IT IS IMPORTANT TO WEIGHT LOSS

When it comes to weight loss, many people think only of white bread and pasta as carbohydrates. However, table sugar, honey, fruit juices, dairy products, beans, and even items labeled whole wheat and whole grain are members of the carbohydrate family. Even though some of these foods have great nutritional value, they still can cause weight gain or reduce the speed of weight loss. To understand why, we need to talk about insulin. The terms insulin and blood sugar matter not only to diabetics but to all of us. Insulin is a hormone that regulates our metabolism, which is the system that burns fat and carbohydrates in the body.

All foods that contain carbohydrates can raise blood glucose. This causes insulin to spike, which promotes fat storage in the body. *But* certain carbohydrates raise blood sugar more than others. For steady weight loss you must stick to foods that will cause the lowest spike in blood sugar. These tend to be animal proteins, including fish and seafood, and non-starchy vegetables.

There are three primary categories of carbohydrates: (1) complex fibrous carbohydrates, (2) starchy complex carbohydrates (wheat and starches), and (3) simple carbohydrates (sugars). Below I have included a breakdown of the primary carbohydrates and an understanding of how they work in the body. Remember, I'm not Dr. Caroline, just Caroline.

CAROLINE'S COMMANDMENT #6

Lean protein and non-starchy vegetables:
Thou shalt have no other foods but me.

CARBOHYDRATES

THE GOOD CARBS

Non-starchy vegetables that fit under the complex fibrous carbohydrates category cause the lowest increases in blood sugar and contain the lowest amounts of sugar and starch. These are the only carbohydrates you should consume if you are trying to lose weight. Fibrous carbohydrates take longer to digest than other carbohydrates and can make you feel full longer and eat less, helping to contribute to weight loss. However, in the fibrous carbohydrate category there are also some high-sugar and high-starch foods that, even though they are loaded with nutrients, won't aid in weight loss. These include fruit, beans, and nuts. Remember: Just because something is healthy does not mean that it will help you lose weight.

Note: Due to the extraordinary variety of these

foods, I cannot list every carbohydrate. Use your better judgment, and conduct additional research so you can be a smart eater.

Vegetable Carbohydrates Good for Weight Loss (Low in Starch, Fat, and Sugar)

- Artichoke
- Asparagus
- Bell pepper
- Broccoli
- Brussels sprouts
- Cabbage
- Cauliflower
- Celery
- Collard greens
- Cucumber
- Eggplant
- Endive
- Green onion
- Kale
- Lettuce
- Mushroom
- Mustard greens
- Onions
- Parsnip
- Spinach
- Swiss chard
- Turnip greens
- Watercress

THE BAD CARBS

High-Starch Vegetables: Carbohydrates That Slow Weight Loss

Not all vegetables are created equally. There are some that are high in starch and can pump the breaks on your weight loss.

Vegetable Carbohydrates Highest in Starch

- Potato (*eat a potato, look like a potato*)
- Carrot
- Pumpkin
- Succotash
- Corn
- Peas
- Yam
- Sweet potato
- Winter squash (e.g., butternut)
- Plantain
- All beans
- All nuts

Although beans and nuts are excellent sources of dietary fiber and protein, they are too high in carbohydrates to provide you with weight loss at the speed you want. Quite frankly, do you know of anyone personally who ate lots of beans and nuts to lose 50 or more pounds? I doubt it. Whenever I ate beans or attempted to have nuts as a "healthy snack," even in small amounts, they caused my weight loss to stall or reverse.

CARBOHYDRATES HIGH IN SUGAR: I DON'T EAT FRUIT

I don't eat fruit. Why? Because it is loaded with sugar. Saying that there is such a thing as a healthy sugar is like saying that there is healthy crack.

When you consume sugar, the body recognizes it as SUGAR—no matter what. There is no filtering system in the body says, "Oh la la, this is fruit sugar or agave sugar from a rain forest. Glad she didn't give us that welfare sugar that's in soda." The body just does not work like that. When you eat sugar—whether it is white table sugar, honey, fruit, or brownies—your insulin spikes, and your body will hold on to existing fat like a hostage. This is why many diabetics are instructed not to eat bananas, pineapples, and other high-sugar fruits. Sure, fruit contains fiber, vitamins, and phytonutrients. But all of these nutrients can be found in equal or greater amounts in vegetable sources WITHOUT the sugar. For example, oranges are not the only source of vitamin C. Bell peppers, broccoli, and spinach contain vitamin C as well. Many think that oranges are the only source of vitamin C because of heavy marketing by Florida's orange growers.

If you are serious about seeing the numbers on the scale go down, then you simply have to cut back on all sugar in your diet. This includes fruit, fruit juice, dried fruit, packaged fruit (canned fruit and fruit cups), table sugar, lactose, agave, and honey.

THE VERY, VERY BAD CARBS

Wheat, rice, sugar, and dairy cause the largest spikes in insulin. And the stronger the insulin spike, the more fat storage (*especially in the abdominal area*), thus making way for rapid weight gain and high triglyceride levels. This is why diabetics are told to reduce these foods. The worst part of eating wheat, flour, rice, sugar and dairy is that they make you want more and more food. Eating them also causes instant adverse changes to your body. The next day, your jeans are a little tighter, or by the end of the day the stomach bulge in your dress looks just a little bigger. These foods have no place in anyone's weight loss plans. Although some have great nutritional value, eating them will cause you to not lose any weight at all or to lose it in super slow motion.

Starchiest Carbohydrates

- Whole wheat and whole grain bread
- Whole wheat pasta and whole grain pasta
- Oatmeal
- Grits
- Pasta
- Brown rice
- Beans
- Potatoes *(eat a potato, look like a potato)*
- Yams
- Corn
- Anything made with flour

Send-Your-Blood-Sugar-Through-the-Roof Carbohydrates

- Milk
- Processed foods *(usually anything in a package or box)*
- White bread
- White pasta
- Dried fruit
- Table sugar
- Honey
- Corn syrup
- High-fructose corn syrup
- Fruit juice *(fresh and concentrate)*
- Most packaged cereal

Whether or not you are a diabetic, one of the major drawbacks of eating these foods is that they are converted into sugar in the body. They may make you feel full at first, but your appetite can quickly rebound so you are even hungrier than before. This is why people often have a once-they-pop-they-can't-stop mentality when they eat things like cake and cookies. For me, it was a gradual process, but once I completely eliminated all sugar, wheat, flour, dairy, and rice from my diet, my weight loss skyrocketed. And I don't say this lightly: I lost weight so consistently that family members actually joked that I was on drugs.

WHEAT: THE HEROIN OF THE FOOD WORLD

If you are still gaining weight even though you exercise regularly; eat plenty of vegetables, whole wheat bread, and whole wheat pasta; and avoid junk food, fast food, and sugary soft drinks, the culprit is likely wheat. Wheat and all the products made from it are the heroin of the food world. Just so we're clear flour comes from wheat.The wheat industry makes the most money on the block, and wheat is the most addictive of the dangerous foods. Fresh-baked bread and pasta give the feeling of euphoria, and people who consume wheat come back again and again. Wheat is an appetite stimulant, and eating it only makes you want more—in higher and more unhealthy doses and forms, such as cupcakes and cookies. And just as drugs have made their way onto almost every doorstep in America, so has wheat. It is in almost everything we eat. Wheat isn't just used to make white bread and white pasta but is used many other items as well.

Foods Containing Wheat

- <u>**All**</u> cereals (and I mean **all cereals**, even the ones that you think are healthy, such as Special K, corn flakes, etc.)

- **<u>All</u>** breads (pita, white bread, whole wheat bread, rye, sourdough, Italian, pumpernickel, poppy seed, biscuits, multigrain, Ezekiel bread)
- **<u>All</u>** pasta (whole wheat, whole grain, white)
- Anything made from a batter (waffles, pancakes)
- Canned soups *(wheat is used to thicken many soups)*
- Crackers
- Gravy mixes and dips
- Vegetarian meat products
- Baked goods (cookies, cakes, pastries, pies, scones, danishes, doughnuts)
- Beer
- Imitation meat products

Instead of an overdose, you get overweight. Wheat is the cause of the pregnancy pouch at the bottom of your stomach (even though you are not even pregnant) and the Goodyear tire around your husband's waist.

PRODUCTS LABELED WHOLE WHEAT AND WHOLE GRAIN

Understanding White Bread vs. Brown (Whole Wheat Bread)

In the current nutrition advice, the light-skinned

side of the family (white bread) is not favored. Whole grain, whole wheat, and multigrain are the "it girls," when, really, they are the *mean girls* in terms of what they do to our body. Heavy marketing makes whole grain, whole wheat, and multigrain look good on the outside, but they are very ugly once inside of you. All foods made from wheat promptly convert to sugar once inside of us, causing huge insulin spikes, which again promotes the storage of fat. Two slices of whole wheat bread will spike your blood sugar more than a candy bar—and, no, that doesn't mean you should eat a candy bar. Bread and other items made from whole wheat, like pasta and crackers—even if they're whole wheat or multigrain—have the same negative effects on weight loss as the white versions. The only difference is that they are less processed and have more nutritional value. Still, more nutritional value does not equal weight loss. A cookie made with whole wheat flour, with the same amount of hydrogenated oils, butter, and sugar, is still a cookie and is like someone trying to offer you a healthy cigarette. So why are whole wheat and whole grain so heavily advertised as healthy? For the same reason everything else in this country is advertised: to make another person rich (the wheat industry) and make you fat and broke for buying it.

Some people complain that when they stop eating wheat, they feel tired, irritable, and unable to function. People who do drugs feel this way when going through detox, but that doesn't mean they need to go back to doing the drug. Similarly, it does not mean you need to go back to eating wheat. Eliminate wheat and sugar in **all** forms from your diet for two to three weeks, and you will be amazed. Over time, you will find that you are in a better mood and even sleep better. Now, if you eliminate wheat but still drink sodas and juices and eat starchy vegetables and other weight-loss stallers, such as fruit, dairy and sweets you will see little to no weight loss. Work your way towards staying free from wheat as long as possible. Re-exposure is like giving drug addicts a taste and expecting them not to relapse.

Foods Labeled Gluten Free. Gluten-free foods are not an alternative to eating wheat. The gluten-free whole grain bread, bagels, crackers, pasta, cereals, and other items seen in grocery stores are made using rice starch, tapioca starch, potato starch, or cornstarch. All of these starches actually trigger even higher blood sugar levels than wheat. These products are marketed to sound healthier, but when it comes to weight loss, they are not. Gluten-free foods are primarily needed for those with celiac disease, a disorder that causes gluten intolerance.

COW'S MILK AND ALL DAIRY PRODUCTS

Yep, cow's milk and all food items containing cow's milk, such as all yogurts, cheese, butter, and sour cream, are members of the very, very bad carbohydrates category. Milk contains lactose, which is a simple sugar. Random fact: Humans are the only creatures on earth that regularly drink another creature's milk. Milk is designed to help baby animals grow and gain weight, and the lactose in it triggers a high insulin response. Calcium can be found in dark, leafy greens (collards, kale, spinach) without the sugar. Also consider this: During pre-historic times and in many current tribal communities, milk or dairy products were not consumed by adults because of the lack of refrigeration. This absence did not stop human evolution.

ALTERNATIVE DAIRY PRODUCTS

There are many alternative dairy products on the market. Think about it this way: Almond milk is made with nuts; soymilk is made with beans; and rice milk is made with rice. Above, I indicated that nuts, rice, and beans are all too high in carbohydrate content for speedy weight loss. Indeed, these alternative milks may be "enriched" with various vitamins and minerals, but yet again remember that this does not equal automatic weight loss. If you are worried about calcium, it can be found in equal or greater value in many deep dark green vegetables.

Where the Very, Very Bad Carbohydrates Hide

Vegetarian and Vegan Meat Products. Most vegetarian and vegan meat products are made using wheat or sugars, or both. It takes a lot of unnatural processes and additives to make a vegetable taste and look like a piece of meat. To do this, sugar, wheat, rice, dairy, excessive salt, or food additives—which are not beneficial to weight loss—are used.

Avoid

- Vegetarian/vegan burgers
- Vegetarian/vegan breakfast sausages
- Vegetarian/vegan hot dogs
- Vegetarian/vegan dairy products (e.g., cheese, sour cream)
- Vegetarian/vegan chicken nuggets
- Vegetarian/vegan bacon

Meat in Salad Bars, Fast Food Joints, Delis, and Restaurants. The chicken breasts with the fake grill marks from the salad bar or a McDonald's salad or sandwich likely taste so juicy and sweet because they were injected with sugar-laden seasonings, nitrates, or preservatives.

Avoid

- Grilled chicken in fast food restaurant salads
- Grilled chicken in salad bars
- Deli/sandwich meat used at sandwich shops

Foods Labeled Sugar Free or Fat Free. Stay away from foods with these labels! To make up for lack of taste in sugar-free products, fat or food additives are often added. Likewise, sugar and artificial flavorings are added to replace the fat in "fat-free" foods.

Foods Labeled Zero Trans Fat. I have seen vending-machine brownies, cookies, and honey buns with the label "zero trans fat," which means no hydrogenated oils. Zero trans fat does not mean no fat or that the product is really healthy. It doesn't mean a free-for-all. Trans fats are typically replaced by more saturated fats, sugars, and hard-to-pronounce food additives.

CAROLINE'S COMMANDMENT #7

Sugar is the crack, not cocaine, of the food world.

SUGAR: THE CRACK, NOT COCAINE, OF THE FOOD WORLD

So maybe your craving for sugar won't make you want to go steal a car radio or knock an old lady over the head. But if you think back hard enough, there were probably times that you ate back-to-back chocolates or a whole tub of ice cream and looked and felt like a crackhead eating it. If you already have an uncontrollable appetite, sugar in any form is one of the worst things you can put in your body. Sprinkling sugar on an existing food addiction and emotional eating worsens the problem. Sugar puts your appetite into overdrive. Your stomach will want to become an equal opportunity employer of more and more sugary and fatty foods and will discriminate against truly healthy food. Just use this logic: If you want to eat foods that don't raise blood sugar, well, then you probably shouldn't put things in your body that contain sugar.

SUGAR'S CODE NAMES

Just like drugs on the street, sugar has code names and hides in the least expected places—like soup, salad dressing, and condiments. **Sugar is not just the white stuff.** For successful weight loss and overall health, sugar needs to be avoided in all forms. Sucrose, the white stuff (aka table sugar), is just one of sugar's many forms. Sugar also includes glucose, agave, fructose (as in fruit sugar), lactose (as in milk), maltose or malts (as in rice malt and honey), jam (contains concentrated juice, which is high in fruit sugar), maple syrup, corn syrup, palm sugar (traditionally used in macrobiotic cooking), and the very deceiving organic brown sugar (which is basically the same as white sugar).

Below, I include a full list of code words for sugar that may appear on food labels. In general, stay away from anything that includes the words *syrup* or *sweetener* or anything ending in *-ose*.

- Agave
- Brown sugar
- Corn sweetener
- Corn syrup and Corn syrup solids
- Dextrin
- Dehydrated cane juice
- Dextr<u>ose</u>
- Fruct<u>ose</u>
- Fruit juice concentrate

- Glucose
- High-fructose corn syrup
- Honey
- Invert sugar
- Lactose
- Maltodextrin
- Maltose
- Malt syrup
- Maple syrup
- Molasses
- Raw sugar
- Rice syrup
- Saccharose
- Sorghum and sorghum syrup
- Sucrose
- Syrup
- Treacle
- Turbinado sugar
- Xylose

TRAINING YOUR BRAIN NOT TO CRAVE SWEET

More than likely, sugar was a VIP at almost every important event in your life. From birthday to graduation cakes, there was cake when babies were born, and there were even cakes and pies when someone died. Treats from our grandparents or our favorite aunt or uncle often came in the form of trips to Dairy Queen or a chocolate candy bar. Childhood Saturday mornings were spent watching cartoons with a huge bowl of sugary cereal in our lap. As adults, many women look to chocolate during a rough menstrual cycle and pints of ice cream once they learn that "He's really not that into you." As a result, the brain and tongue become trained to expect high levels of sugar. Just as you may have been trained to crave sweet, you can train yourself not to crave sweet. When I share my eating style, people often ask, "What do you do when you want something sweet?" The answer is I do nothing; it wasn't easy, but I have trained myself to not be the sugar fiend that I once was.

TIPS ON TRAINING YOURSELF NOT TO CRAVE SWEET

- **Don't look to fruit or sugar substitutes to satisfy sweet craving.** Eating something sweet, whether it is from natural or artificial sugar or fruit, only makes the body crave more sweets. Additionally, eating anything sweet actually increases your appetite. Pay attention to your body next time after having a sugar substitute or eating an orange or an apple. You will notice that you still feel hungry.
- **Go gangsta, go cold turkey.** If you cut ALL sugar, sugar substitutes, and sweet-tasting foods from your diet for two weeks, you won't crave sugar as much. This includes all the types of sugar listed under "Sugar's Code Names."

- **Eat protein every 2 to 3 hours.** Skipping meals and not preparing or planning meals ahead of time will set you up to reach for whatever food may be available when you are hungry. In many cases that will be something convenient and sugary like a six-pack of mini-doughnuts from the office vending machine. Keep protein sources like scrambled egg whites and pieces of cooked skinless chicken breasts in your fridge at home and at work. Also, you can keep both canned tuna and salmon packed in water inside your desk at work.
- **If you do give in to the sugar gods, make sure it's worth it.** Instead of having a sugary item that comes out of a package, like a candy bar, go for something homemade. This could be an item from a local bakery, a shared dessert at a quality restaurant, or a small baked good made by a family member. Do this no more than once a week if you are truly trying to wean yourself off of sugar.
- **Lose the change.** If you are the fan club president of the office vending machine, clean out all of the loose change and single dollar bills in your purse so that you are less likely to buy

anything from the vending machine. Also, clean out the loose change that may be in your car's ashtray or the bottom of your purse to prevent you from buying a sugary drink or shake at a fast food drive-thru. If you have a habit of stopping to get fast food or sugary items on your way home from work, eat a small meal of lean protein and non-starchy vegetables right before you leave work.

- **Wait out the craving.** Unlike illicit drug cravings, sugar cravings last only a couple of minutes. Find something else to do for a good 10 to 15 minutes, and the craving will more than likely pass. Examples are dancing like a video girl around your house, finding something to organize, standing on your front porch or balcony in the cold for a few minutes, or looking at old fat pictures of yourself.
- **Don't put yourself in the crack house.** Respectfully decline invitations to dessert and cupcake tasting events. Temptation will kick your butt. Also, if you must go to a work or family event where you know there will be a huge dessert spread, don't allow yourself to even walk by or see the dessert spread. Have someone else

make you a plate of lean meat and non-starchy vegetables if possible.

- **Living without sugar will get easier.** If you cut all things sweet from your diet for two weeks, you won't crave them as much.

MY THOUGHTS ON MODERATION

Some have suggested that I recommend moderation instead of complete elimination of certain foods because it is more realistic. Again, my advice is not based on the realistic versus unrealistic but what I did to be successful at weight loss. If you truly believe that you are a food addict, especially when it comes to sugar, or are 100 pounds over your normal body weight, you do not have the self-discipline to "just have a little." I am not saying that you never will, but if you are just beginning your weight loss journey, I guarantee that you don't. It will happen over time. Also, merely cutting back on rice, dairy, sugar, grain, wheat and flour will not give you the instant weight loss results you want to stay motivated. *And then you will be telling your friends that my weight loss manual did not help you lose any weight.* People are forced to eliminate alcohol, cigarettes, and drugs in efforts to save their lives; certain foods should not be any different. Last time I checked, the number of people dying from obesity-related ailments was neck and neck with, if not greater than, the number of those dying of illnesses related to the use of alcohol, cigarettes, or drugs. I'm just sayin'. As my mother often says, "Rome was not built in a day." Eliminating foods that you have been eating for decades won't happen overnight—it certainly did not for me—so make it a gradual process. The more I removed sugar and carbohydrates from my diet, the more. I could see results in how my clothes no longer fit. May sound a lil' superficial, but this is what kept me motivated.

DRUM ROLL . . . ALCOHOL

Pure alcohol is not a sugar, but when it gets inside of the body it acts like a sugar. When we drink alcohol, the body detects it as a poison and makes every effort to get rid of it. In doing this, the body stops focusing on producing insulin, and it negatively affects the body's blood sugar levels. This also causes the metabolism (the body's fat-burning system) to slow down. Wine and alcoholic drinks mixed with concentrated juices elevate this problem even more because of the combination of alcohol and sugar entering the body. As little as 2 ounces of alcohol can throw your blood sugar out of whack. Also, we lose our inhibitions when we drink. When we're buzzed or pissy drunk, we forget our weight loss goals and eat late-night pancakes, burgers, and deep-fried foods.

Full disclosure: Did I drink during my weight loss journey? Yes. Not only did drinking alcohol cause intermittent weight loss stalls, but it often heightened feelings of sadness, a lack of self-worth, and depression. If you truly believe that you are an emotional eater, food addict, or any other kind of addict, drinking alcohol is like putting your addiction and emotions on steroids. Alcohol should not be a participant in weight loss. Making "healthy drinking recommendations" is an oxymoron. But I also feel like leaving readers without any healthy alcohol tips—to keep weight, hangovers, and worse away—would be like pushing a person into the ocean without a life jacket. So here they are:

DRINKING TIPS

- Stick to red wine or diet soda and vodka, if you want a cocktail. They are lowest in sugar and carbohydrate content.
- If your drink matches any color in the rainbow, it is likely loaded with sugar.

- Never trust a man who orders flavored vodka.
- If a stranger offers to buy you a drink, go with him to get your drink from the bar. Don't stay on the dance floor or lounge area waiting for him to bring your drink back.
- Brown liquor will only make you forget where you live.
- Champagne is just ginger ale that knows somebody.
- Always have a balanced meal before having drinks.
- Every drink should be followed by at least one cup of water.
- Know your limits. No one thinks that the drunk bitch in the club is cute.
- Think beer, think beer belly.
- Consume non-alcoholic beverages during and after exercise. Eat a full meal, and wait a little while before hitting the bar after your gym workout.
- Remember, all things in moderation. Always have a designated driver, and keep in mind that taxis run all night.

CAROLINE'S COMMANDMENT #8

Black girls shouldn't eat carbs.

What I have learned about sugar and carbohydrates is that black girls shouldn't eat them. Yeah, I said it. I actually considered this as a title for this book. This book is not intended for only one specific race. However, I can speak on weight loss only from the perspective of a black woman, because I am, well, African-American and Guyanese. I also can't speak for the weight loss challenges and experiences of all black women. However, I can say this: After years of trying every single diet, program, plan, and fad, the only method that worked was eating a diet devoid of the following carbohydrates: rice, wheat, flour, grain, sugar, and dairy. Similarly, all of the black women I have met who have lost 50 to 100 pounds without weight loss surgery also say that they were only able to lose weight by cutting rice, wheat, flour, grain, sugar, and dairy from their diet.

BIO-INDIVIDUALITY: BLACK GIRLS AND CARBS

When it comes to black women and weight loss, we face one of the toughest foes in history: genetics. Women of African descent tend naturally to carry more weight in their midsection, hips, butt, and thighs. Foods containing sugar, wheat, flour, rice, grain, or dairy tend to immediately add more bulk to our already-thick midsections. I'm not saying that this does not happen to women of other races, but our bodies tend to hold on to that extra bulk pretty tightly and for longer periods. And, FYI, there is no such thing as being "big-boned." This was just your grandmother's way of saying "fat" without hurting your feelings. For black girls wanting to lose weight, eating rice, wheat, flour, grain, sugar, and dairy is like adding lighter fluid to a fire. This includes foods made with whole wheat, brown rice, whole grain, and multigrains. Yeah, you may have heard this stuff is healthy, but from whom? More than likely, the morning show nutritionist or health magazine blogger/intern/Tweeter whose salary is being supported by the manufacturer of the whole wheat or whole grain product advertised. Also, quite frankly, that person likely does not have saddlebag hips that just won't go away or belly flab hanging over her vagina. Meaning they are most likely not currently morbidly obese and never have been.

The idea that black women should not eat carbohydrates is not so far-fetched. *Bio-individuality* means different foods are best for different people based on factors such as lifestyle, age, gender, blood type, and even ancestry. The concept suggests that one person's food is another person's poison. This is why diets that work for some may not work well for others. This is how we can have friends who eat whatever they want and gain no weight, while if we even look at a slice of pizza, we gain 5 pounds. Ethnic groups are diverse—and so should be our approaches to weight loss.

Understand that there is no one way of eating that works perfectly for everybody. In terms of bio-individuality and blacks, perhaps low-carbohydrate and dairy-free diets work best because in many traditional communities in Africa, where dairy was not easily accessible or easy to store in the heat, people thrived on animal protein and vegetables. Of course, there were also no processed foods because the machines to create them were not accessible or had not been invented. Additionally, like many black people, my blood type is O, and there is research that suggests that type O's feel more energized by eating meat. Just a theory.

Lastly, black women, let's not praise morbid obesity with terms such as "large and in charge," "big and beautiful," or "fat and fabulous," nor believe that the terms "thick" and "overweight" are interchangeable. Indeed, real women have curves, but real women also put their health before beauty.

EAT MEAT . . . AND SEAFOOD!

Animal protein and seafood have virtually no effect on blood sugar, and in essence are the only naturally carbohydrate-free foods. However, like vegetables, not all animal proteins are created equal in the world of weight loss. Although chicken wings and thighs, beef, and pork are loaded with protein, their high fat content always caused my weight loss to stall or go into reverse. When I stuck to eating leaner sources of protein, such as skinless chicken and turkey breasts, egg whites, and seafood, I lost more weight and felt less sluggish, and my skin looked great.

Consider lean protein as an appetite suppressant. The term "protein" is constantly used in food marketing, yet many don't know why protein is important. Protein is essential to shedding pounds for two reasons: (1) Eating protein suppresses the hunger hormone ghrelin.

When we eat protein it sends a message from our gut to our brain that says, "Hey, I'm full." (2) Also, eating lean protein helps to sustain lean muscle mass. Retaining muscle mass is important because muscle burns fat and helps to keep your metabolism elevated. Focus on getting your lean protein from natural whole foods such as lean meat (skinless chicken breasts, turkey breasts, egg whites) and seafood. Don't look for protein in nutrition bars, cereals, protein powders, or protein drinks. These are all processed foods that often contain added sugar and chemical-like ingredients. Also, these processed forms of synthetic protein can cause kidney problems.

DON'T BE AFRAID OF FAT!

THE FAT YOU NEED

For weight loss, stick mostly to polyunsaturated fats and monounsaturated fats. These fats typically come from vegetables or fish sources. However, just as with every other food category, some of the sources of polyunsaturated and monounsaturated fats, such as nuts, beans, corn, and certain oils, must be prohibited in the name of weight loss.

Polyunsaturated Fat. Stick to getting polyunsaturated fat from seafood high in omega-3 fatty acids. You must aim for eating fish high in omega-3 fatty acids a few times a week. Otherwise you will feel as if you are going to fall out and can't function. Your body needs fat—just healthy fat. If your budget permits, aim for eating a source of omega-3–rich seafood daily. The oils in fish help to decrease insulin levels and boost your metabolism. Also, you will feel full longer and not crave "feel good" comfort foods. Still, seafood can be expensive. As an alternative, purchase frozen seafood in bulk from warehouse stores. You can also try taking a tablespoon a day of liquid omega-3 oil or cod-liver oil that is refrigerated in most health food stores. The fish oil capsules that sit unrefrigerated on drugstore and grocery store shelves are less potent. If you do buy the fish oil capsules, be sure to keep them refrigerated.

Fish and Seafood High in Omega-3 Fatty Acids

- Salmon
- Anchovies
- Bluefin tuna
- Sardines
- Trout
- Crab
- Cod
- Scallops
- Lobster
- Halibut
- Shrimp

Salmon is my favorite. I eat salmon before every workout, and it makes me feel like I'm going as fast as Flo Jo when I run. Also, after my workouts I don't feel as ravenous if I've eaten salmon before the workout. Sometimes I even have a salmon filet for breakfast. It makes me feel full and prepared for my day, like the kids in those Chex commercials.

Monounsaturated Fat. These fats are deemed as healthy fats since they help to reduce cholesterol levels. These fats are primarily found in oils, such as pure extra virgin olive oil and even some seafood sources such as Atlantic pickled herring, halibut, sablefish, and mackerel.

THE FAT YOU DON'T NEED

Saturated Fat. This fat is often found in pork, beef, chicken skin, and processed foods. Too much saturated fat in a person's diet increases the risk for heart disease and raises cholesterol. Nope, I don't know this from a research study but from firsthand experience. During my days of trying every fad diet on the market, I tried Atkins. I was eating beef, pork, chicken wings, and full-fat cheese. I lost weight at first, but it eventually stopped. Then during a routine physical, my doctor informed me that my cholesterol levels were off the charts, and she told me that other patients who did Atkins encountered the same problem. Many supporters of Atkins and low-carb diets suggest that saturated fat is healthy and act like Tea Party protestors when anyone challenges them. Again, there is no one-size-fits-all approach. If some are truly able to eat saturated fat, lose weight, and remain in good health, so be it. Perhaps it goes back to my bio-individuality that, as a black person, I am predisposed to heart disease or high cholesterol levels. What I do know is that when I stopped eating saturated fat, my cholesterol levels went down, my skin was clearer, and my weight loss picked back up.

Trans Fat. Trans fat is the bastard child of sugar. This type of fat is more detrimental to your health than butter. Eating trans fat can take your bad cholesterol levels through the roof, and it increases your risk for coronary heart disease. Trans fats are commonly found in margarine, shortening, breakfast cereals, fried foods, crackers, potato chips, and packaged pastries, cookies, doughnuts, cakes, and pies.

CHAPTER 3

HOW I ATE TO LOSE MY FIRST 100 POUNDS

AT MY CATHOLIC grade school, math was never my favorite subject, and I even waited until my senior year of college to complete my math requirement. So adopting a style of eating that would require me to count calories, measurements, or portions just would not have been a good match. Also, my father is from Guyana, and when he made dinner, every meal included fresh meat or seafood and food that I had to chew. I grew up eating food that had a mother! Therefore, a diet that was essentially vegetarian or that replaced meals with liquid shakes or smoothies was out of the question. Realistic and sustainable weight loss occurs only when people are met where they are and based on who they are.

Here is my approach to eating for weight loss: Forget calories. Think categories.

- Eat only from these two categories: 1) lean proteins, and 2) non-starchy vegetables.
- Eat every 2 to 3 hours.
- Drink half your body weight in ounces of water each day. For example, if you weigh 200 pounds, drink 100 ounces of water a day.
- Dine out once a week, staying within these two categories. *(No worries, I provide tips on how to do this.)*

I focus on eating until I am no longer physically hungry. What I absolutely do not eat is: wheat, flour, sugar, rice, dairy, fruit, nuts, and beans. Eating this way has been the key factor in maintaining my 150-pound weight loss. In addition to sustaining my weight loss, again, this method of healthy eating has not killed me or caused any health problems.

Below, I have included a breakdown of acceptable and unacceptable foods. If it's not listed here or if it's listed as unacceptable, don't eat it! Many of the items on the unacceptable lists are nutritious, but they can stall weight loss—and healthy weight loss is your goal. I also include meal plans.

COOKING METHODS

Cook your food naked. This does not mean cook your food without seasonings, but focus on sugarless, dry seasonings such as herbs and spices. So many liquid marinades, gravies, barbeque and pasta sauces, and mixes are loaded with hidden grains, sugars, and unnecessary food additives. Always read labels when buying a seasoning to ensure it does not contain sugar, sugar code names, dairy, wheat, or flour. Flour is used as a thickener for many sauces. To make your food more flavorful, marinate with dry seasonings in a sealable plastic bag the night before cooking.

Cook your own food 90 percent of the time. Just because you buy food at a health food store or a fancy restaurant does not mean the meal is healthy or will aid in your weight loss. Menus do not always list all food ingredients. There are often hidden sugars and processed oils used in cooking, seasonings, and marinades. The only way to know exactly what you are eating 90 percent of the time is if you cook, not microwave, your food yourself.

ACCEPTABLE COOKING METHODS

- Broiling
- Baking
- Grilling

- Searing
- Steaming
- Poaching
- Boiling

Use only the acceptable oils listed below. Invest in high-quality nonstick cookware, and you will need almost no oil at all.

UNACCEPTABLE COOKING METHODS

- Frying
- Deep-frying (especially breaded items)
- Cooking in cream
- Au gratin

OILS

ACCEPTABLE OILS

- Oil should not be necessary, especially if you are using high-quality nonstick cookware.
- If needed, use Pam cooking spray with no more than 1 to 2 sprays.
- Also, no more than 2 teaspoons of **pure** extra virgin olive oil or grape seed oil labeled "cold pressed" or "expeller pressed" is allowed each day.

- 1 teaspoon of flaxseed oil or fish oil daily is recommended, not for cooking but for overall health.

UNACCEPTABLE OILS

- Soybean oil
- Canola oil (other than the 1 to 2 sprays of Pam cooking spray)
- Coconut oil
- Sesame oil
- Safflower oil
- Walnut oil

Note: Due to the extraordinary variety of these foods, I cannot list every food in these categories. Use your better judgment based on the previous nutritional information provided.

LEAN PROTEINS

ACCEPTABLE LEAN PROTEINS

- Egg whites
- Skinless chicken and turkey breasts
- All fish, shellfish, and seafood. *Salmon is particularly good because its healthy omega-3 fat will*

keep you satiated. Canned fish is good if it's packed in water, not oil.

UNACCEPTABLE PROTEINS

- Beef
- Pork
- Duck
- Game meats
- Lamb
- Chicken wings and thighs
- Whole eggs
- Egg beaters or egg substitutes (these are processed foods)
- Canned meat
- Vegetarian meat substitutes
- Luncheon meats (bologna, salami, packed turkey)
- Prepackaged smoked or cured salmon (these are usually injected with sugar for flavoring)
- Nuts or nut butters
- Beans (dried or canned)

VEGETABLES

Tip: Eat raw, dark leafy greens every day, or eat other acceptable vegetables raw as much as possible. It will provide more nutrients and keep your energy elevated.

ACCEPTABLE VEGETABLES

- Mushrooms
- Cauliflower
- Cabbage
- Brussels sprouts
- Spinach
- Kale
- Broccoli
- Arugula
- Avocados

These are just examples, and there are many more vegetables that promote weight loss not on this list. Eating vegetables every day is very important. The nutrients keep your energy level up, and prevent constipation.

TIPS ON BUYING FRESH VEGETABLES

- Do not purchase produce that is bruised or damaged or looks like it has fallen off the back of a truck.
- When selecting fresh-cut produce—such as pre-chopped celery sticks or bagged salad greens—choose items that are refrigerated or surrounded by ice.

- Bag fresh fruits and vegetables separately from meat, poultry, and seafood products.

Still, buying fresh produce and eating it before it begins to spoil can be difficult. Therefore, I recommend buying frozen vegetables. Not only do frozen vegetables last longer than fresh ones, they tend to be less expensive, and they are already sliced or diced.

In many cases frozen vegetables are higher in nutrients than fresh vegetables. Vegetables selected for freezing are usually picked when they are at their peak ripeness and the most nutritious. Immediately after being picked, they are flash-frozen, which allows them to retain much of their nutrition.

TIPS ON BUYING AND COOKING FROZEN VEGETABLES

- Avoid frozen, prepared vegetable dishes with dairy-based sauces.
- Read labels: Some frozen vegetables have added fat, sugar, and salt. You don't want to use those.
- Don't cook frozen vegetables until they're lifeless—the way your aunt cooks greens at Thanksgiving.
- Vegetables should be slightly crisp when you eat them.

- Don't defrost frozen vegetables before cooking.

UNACCEPTABLE VEGETABLES

- Corn
- Peas
- Carrots
- Yucca
- Plantains
- Beets
- Squash
- Pumpkin
- Okra
- Potatoes
- Sweet potatoes
- Canned vegetables. *Canned vegetables are a no-no. They go through a preservation process very different from frozen vegetables, which drains them of most of their nutrients.*

CONDIMENTS

ACCEPTABLE CONDIMENTS

- All herbs and spices, including salt and pepper.

- Fresh salsa in the refrigerated section of the grocery store, not jarred
- Vinegar (white wine, red wine, and balsamic)
- Mustard
- Hot sauce (read label to check for sugar content)

UNACCEPTABLE CONDIMENTS

- Liquid marinades
- Honey mustard
- Chutney
- Concentrated lemon and lime juice
- Mayonnaise (regular and fat-free)
- Barbeque sauce
- Tomato or pasta sauce
- Mint sauce
- Ketchup
- Lemon pepper
- Thick, creamy salad dressings
- Jellies and preserves
- Teriyaki sauce
- Tartar sauce
- Sweet pickles
- Steak sauce
- Worcestershire sauce
- Prepackaged vinaigrettes. *Even though you may*

have heard that vinaigrettes are "healthy," many are made with sugar and hydrogenated oils. If you can't see through your salad dressing, you shouldn't use it. You can find recipes online to make your own sugarless vinaigrettes at home. Combining vinegar and a sugarless mustard is an easy way to make vinaigrette.

DRINKS

ACCEPTABLE DRINKS

- Water. *To determine your daily water intake (in ounces), divide your body weight by two. For example, if you weigh 300 pounds, you should drink 150 ounces of water each day. If you are an avid exerciser who sweats like a horse when you work out, drink an extra 30 ounces of water daily. Keep gallon jugs of water in your car and near your bed, computer, television, and desk so you always have access to water.*
- Coffee and tea. *Green tea, herbal tea, and decaffeinated coffee are okay. For some people, caffeine can trigger food cravings or stall weight loss.* When drinking caffeine, monitor your food cravings and also evaluate if the caffeine may be causing your weight loss to stall

UNACCEPTABLE DRINKS

- Soda
- Juice. *When fruit is juiced, the fiber is removed. Even with no sugar added, apple, grape, orange, and cherry juices have the same amount of sugar as sodas.*
- Diet soda and diet juice. *The sugar substitutes stall weight loss and cause hunger cravings.*
- Smoothies
- Coconut water
- Energy drinks
- Flavored water
- Alcohol. *Besides adding empty calories, alcohol can impair your judgment of food choices. Tell yourself it's not really worth it. Don't be dependent on alcohol for fun.*
- Sweetened coffees, mixed coffee drinks, and sweetened teas

SNACKS

The principles for snacking are the same as for meals. Stick to the acceptable foods. First, you have to recognize that snacks are not a constitutional right. Constant snacking is one of the main reasons that diets fail. Even allegedly healthy snacks like almonds can lead to a once-you-pop-you-can't-stop mentality. Although this section is labeled snacks, think about these snacks as smaller meals of lean protein and non-starchy vegetables to have throughout the day. At the beginning of each week stock up on these foods in your home and office. This way you will have access to lean protein and non-starchy vegetables at all times.

ACCEPTABLE SNACKS

- Skinless boneless chicken breasts (after cooked and cooled, put in a sealable sandwich bag to break into chunks)
- Cans of tuna or salmon packed in water
- Scrambled egg whites
- Leftover lean protein and non-starchy vegetables from lunch or dinner
- Sliced cucumber (soak overnight in vinegar and acceptable dry seasonings)
- Celery sticks with hot sauce (look for low-sodium hot sauce, and read labels to ensure they contain no sugar)
- Strips of bell peppers (red, green, orange, or yellow) (soak overnight in vinegar and acceptable dry seasonings)
- Cooked shrimp or mini-shrimp cocktail (sometimes in grocery stores) (do not eat the cocktail sauce because it contains sugar)

UNACCEPTABLE SNACKS

- Any foods from the unacceptable lists
- Anything in a box
- Foods made with sugar, sugar code names, flour, wheat, dairy, fruit, rice, or beans
- Nuts and seeds
- Chips, crackers, and cookies (potato chips, tortilla chips, veggie chips, 100-calorie pack products)
- Dried fruit and fruit snacks
- Energy drinks, meal replacement bars or drinks, and smoothies

SUBSTITUTIONS FOR CARBOHYDRATES

Rice Craving—Chop uncooked cauliflower until it looks like grains of rice. Stir-fry in one of the acceptable oils.

Mashed Potato Craving—Blend cooked cauliflower in a blender or food processor until it has a whipped texture.

Fried Foods Craving—Coat an acceptable lean protein with ground flaxseed and Pam cooking spray, cooking at 350 degrees and flipping the meat after 30 to 35 minutes. The crunchy exterior will resemble fried foods.

Noodle Craving—Stir-fry shredded cabbage with an acceptable lean protein and oil. This can give you the feeling of chow mein.

GENERALLY UNACCEPTABLE FOODS

I can't cover every food in the world in my lists, so you will sometimes have to use your own best judgment. Here are some additional guiding principles about what to avoid.

SUGAR AND SUGAR SUBSTITUTES

Once something sweet is eaten, whether it is sweetened with natural sugar or an artificial sweetener, the human body automatically craves more sweets—and more food in general. It's easy to fall into the trap of feeling safe with sugar substitutes or types of sugar that we don't recognize as sugar!

AVOID DAIRY

No dairy in any form is allowed. This includes:

- Yogurt (Greek or regular)
- Cow's milk in any form (skim, 2 percent, whole)
- Ice cream

- Cheese
- Dairy-based sauces like Alfredo
- Fat-free dairy products
- Butter
- Cream cheese
- Dairy spreads
- Frozen yogurt
- Creamer (including non-fat)
- Powdered milk, ice milk
- Any processed foods made with dairy

All dairy contains lactose, which is a form of sugar. Remember, there is no healthy sugar! Sugar is sugar is sugar. Milk is not the only option for calcium. No one food has a monopoly on a nutrient—there are always alternatives.

AVOID THESE CARBOHYDRATES

- Rice (white, brown, multigrain, etc.)
- Whole grains
- Wheat (white and whole wheat)
- Flour
- Pasta (white and whole wheat)
- All cereals
- Oatmeal
- Whole grain snack bars
- Granola bars

CHAPTER 4

THE RIGHT STUFF: BUYING AND PLANNING HEALTHY MEALS

LET'S SHOP!

WAREHOUSE STORES AND GROCERY STORES

For healthy food items I shop at a combination of warehouse stores, such as Costco and Sam's Club, and regular grocery stores. Making trips to two places to buy food may seem tedious, but it helped saved money and assured that the healthy items I needed were always fully stocked. It can be overwhelming to shop in the best of circumstances. Use my shopping lists as guides to ensure you have the acceptable foods to begin your weight loss journey.

Warehouse Store Shopping List

- 2 bags of frozen, uncooked chicken breasts (unseasoned)
- 1 bag of frozen, uncooked medium shrimp (unseasoned)
- 2 bags of frozen, uncooked, individually wrapped salmon filets (unseasoned)
- 1 large bag of frozen green beans
- 1 bag of frozen, uncooked scallops
- Cooking spray
- Extra virgin olive oil
- Canned tuna and salmon packed in water
- Powdered garlic
- Minced fresh garlic
- Powdered onion
- Sea salt
- Parsley
- Rosemary
- Red pepper flakes
- Salt-free seasoning

Regular Grocery Store Shopping List

- Ground chicken or turkey breasts. *Read the label. If it does not say breasts, then don't buy it. It must say breasts, not just lean. Some varieties of ground chicken or turkey breasts say "made with rib meat." Stay away from these as they contain unnecessary fat.*

- 3 pounds of frozen snow crab legs
- Frozen vegetables (Brussels sprouts, French-style green beans, green peppers, onions, kale, and cauliflower)
- Fresh vegetables. *Buy no more than 1 bag of salad greens and shredded red and white cabbage, which is not just for coleslaw—it can be cooked as a side dish. Only 1 bag is suggested because it spoils fast.*
- Fresh salsa. *Check the refrigerated section. Do not buy jarred salsa because it usually contains corn syrup and other unhealthy additives.*
- Variety of seasonings
- 1 bag of ground flaxseed meal—only seed recommended

LOCAL FARMERS' MARKETS

I often buy produce from local farmers' markets instead of the grocery store. The offerings at farmers' markets come from local farmers, so they don't go through a long travel process. For the most part the farmers' market offerings tend to be bigger, taste better, and cost less than those from the grocery store. (Most vendors will let you sample and don't charge sales tax.) Also, small and local farmers tend to **not** use the chemicals on their produce that the big grocery store produce suppliers use.

GROCERY STORES IN THE HOOD

I may receive some backlash for this. During my weight loss journey and even now I shop for healthy items at grocery stores in the hood, or what are known as "bad neighborhoods" because of high crime rates. Foods like spinach, shredded cabbage, white and red wine vinegar, and dry seasonings (like rosemary and thyme) are always—and I mean always—on sale, likely because not many people in the hood are buying them. However, I don't buy meat or seafood in the hood: They never look or smell great. Of course, if you plan to visit the hood to grocery shop, do it in the early morning for safety reasons.

DISCOUNT STORES (DOLLAR STORES)

Additionally, you will need durable containers and other items to plan your meals ahead of time. The best places to find cheap reuseable containers and other kitchen items are dollar stores. I find that they are cheaper than Walmart. Depending on where you are located, stick to the Family Dollar chain. Those stores tend to carry more of the name brand quality items, versus the generic containers, which often leak.

Discount Store Shopping List

- Reuseable plastic containers
- Plastic bags
- Nonstick cookware
- Insulated lunch bag

HEALTHY MEALS AND EATING

Eat with the frequency of a newborn baby. Eat mini-meals of lean protein and non-starchy vegetables every 2 to 3 hours. Eating this often actually increases your metabolism and feeds muscle and starves fat. Remember: The more muscle you have, the faster the metabolism. Skipping meals or trying to have just one meal a day causes the body to go into survival mode and hold on to existing fat because it doesn't know when you will feed it again.

Every meal should consist of an acceptable lean protein and an acceptable vegetable. Keep it simple. Here are a few meal-planning tips to remember:

Prepare or know what your three main meals for the day will be ahead of time. You should prepare enough of each meal so that you could have two servings. Preparing enough for two servings at dinner is helpful because it gives you the option of having leftovers for breakfast or already having a lunch prepared for the next day. Cook meals ahead of time, and put them in microwavable containers.

Eat the same basic breakfast every day. Mornings are hard enough without also having to figure out what you should eat. Every morning I eat egg-white omelets, scrambled egg whites, egg-white frittatas, or dinner leftovers.

No time to make breakfast in the morning? Make omelets at night, and nuke them in the microwave in the morning. Eat while you are ironing your clothes and watching the news.

Take your own lunch to work each day. I often carry a bag of prewashed salad greens and whatever lean protein I had for dinner the previous night. I store my salad vineagar in the office fridge. Make enough lunch so that you can eat two lunches a day. This prevents feeling ravenously hungry when you get home. If you are an after-work exerciser, this ensures that you have the proper nutrients before your workout.

Remember to drink half your body weight in

ounces of water each day. For example, if you weigh 200 pounds, you need to drink 100 ounces of water a day to fully flush fat out of your body. Your intake of coffee and tea does not count as part of your water intake.

Eat a lot of the same foods. Trying to incorporate a variety of foods can become time consuming and expensive and make sticking to healthy eating difficult. For me, I stuck to eating a lot of the same foods, such as chicken breasts, salads, egg whites, salmon, and dark leafy greens that I made myself at home. I always knew what my go-to foods would be. For more recipes, visit my website, www.CarolineJhingory.com

Have seafood or breakfast for dinner. Since the metabolism is slowest around dinnertime, your final meal should not be heavy. Often for dinner I will have an egg-white omelet or salmon and spinach salad. Think of it like this: Eat breakfast like a king, eat lunch like a prince, and eat dinner like a pauper.

Below, I have included examples of my meals:

Example #1

8:00 a.m. – Half an egg-white omelet with red bell peppers (save the other half)

- Again, I don't measure, so pour in enough egg whites to make a medium-size omelet in a skillet heated with Pam cooking spray.

11:00 a.m. – Other half of the egg-white omelet with red bell peppers

12:30 p.m. – A few pieces of shredded chicken breasts and celery sticks, cucumbers, or strips of bell peppers

- Shredded chicken breasts are made by putting cooked chicken breasts in a bag and breaking them into little pieces. Pre-sliced celery sticks, cucumbers, and strips of bell peppers can be found in most grocery stores, or you can buy them whole and slice them at home.

2:00 p.m. – Lunch: Tuna salad (canned tuna, white wine vinegar, diced onions, and celery) wrapped in romaine lettuce

- In a medium bowl, I combine two cans of white albacore tuna, ¼ cup of white wine vinegar, and finely diced onions and celery, and mix. Refrigerator overnight and stuff into romaine lettuce leaves for eating.

5:00 p.m. – One additional tuna salad and romaine lettuce wrap before leaving work

7:30 – 8:00 p.m. – Salmon and roasted Brussels sprouts drizzled with balsamic vinegar

- Coat salmon with salt and pepper and cook on both sides in a skillet greased with Pam cooking spray. Chop Brussels sprouts in half or finely. Place in an oven-safe dish with acceptable oil and drizzle with balsamic vinegar. Bake in a 350-degree oven for about 7 to 10 minutes.

Example #2

8:00 a.m. – Half an egg-white frittata with fresh salsa (save the other half)

11:00 a.m. – Other half of the egg-white frittata with fresh salsa

12:30 p.m. – One can of salmon packed in water or shredded skinless chicken breasts and celery sticks, cucumbers in vinegar, or strips of bell peppers

2:00 p.m. – Garlicky kale with turkey breast cutlets

5:00 p.m. – Garlicky kale with turkey breast cutlets

7:30 – 8:00 p.m. – Cod dipped in egg whites and coated with chopped herbs and then baked, served with green beans

Example #3

8:00 a.m. – Dinner leftovers: ground turkey breast meatballs bound with egg whites and ground flaxseed (not bread crumbs), reheated in the microwave

11:00 a.m. – Crab salad (crab meat, chopped cucumbers, vinegar, and chopped green onion)

2:00 p.m. – Crab salad (crab meat, chopped cucumbers, vinegar, and chopped green onion)

5:00 – 6:00 p.m. – Green and red bell peppers stuffed with ground chicken breasts and mushrooms

7:30 – 8:00 p.m. – Egg-white omelet, if still hungry

Example #4

8:00 a.m. – Half of a breakfast scramble of leftover salmon, mushrooms, and egg whites

11:00 a.m. – The rest of the breakfast scramble of leftover salmon, mushrooms, and egg whites

2:00 p.m. – A half-package of prepackaged salad greens, shredded chicken breasts, with red or white wine vinegar as salad dressing

5:00 p.m. – The rest of the salad greens, shredded chicken breasts, with red or white wine vinegar as salad dressing.

7:30 – 8:00 p.m. – Steamed shrimp and string beans seasoned with minced garlic and red pepper

Example #5

8:00 a.m. – Scrambled egg whites with spinach

11:00 a.m. – Canned salmon packed in water or shredded skinless chicken breasts; celery sticks; cucumbers in vinegar or strips of bell peppers

12:30 – 1:00 p.m. – Lunch at a Mexican restaurant: chicken fajitas without the tortilla, with a side salad or a "salad bowl" without the tortilla, corn, beans, or rice. If full, save the other half. Maybe order an extra salad to go for dinner.

4:30 p.m. – Eat to-go Mexican salad until full.

7:30 – 8:00 p.m. – Have the rest of the Mexican salad or roasted scallops and asparagus.

SAFE EATING ON THE GO

I strongly advise that you stick to preparing your meals ahead of time and bringing them with you. However, life happens. Sometimes you forget your packed insulated lunch bag or can't get to the shredded chicken waiting for you in the fridge. In that case, here are my two—yes, only two—go-to spots:

- Grocery store salad bar (make a salad that adheres to the acceptable food guidelines)
- Peruvian chicken eateries. These are popping up in more and more places. The chicken here is cooked similarly to rotisserie style. Order in these exact words: "half chicken white meat and double side salad."

DINE OUT ONCE A WEEK!

Eat out once a week or once every two weeks at a non-buffet style restaurant, not at the home of friends or family. Consider this the 10 percent left over from cooking your own food 90 percent of the time. It may sound like a contradiction from my previous advice, but I suggest this because going out to have a healthy meal provides a change from continually eating at home and perhaps your desk at work. This can cause some people to feel as if they are being punished and will cause episodes of food binging and eating everything in sight. Still, do not waver on the healthy eating rules provided. Also, I recommend eating at non-buffet style restaurants because single-plate restaurants provide a controlled setting. Additionally, I am against dining out at the homes of friends or family because when in the comfort of someone's home, the food is usually self-serve, multiple portions are accessible, and there are usually lots of leftovers waiting to be taken home.

Eating out is fun, and you deserve that. Also, when eating in front of people, most of us tend to not go crazy and pig out. Clearly, the restaurant industry was not created around my healthy eating philosophies, so even with the recommendations below there may be some minor deviations from the acceptable food rules. They won't throw you off the weight loss track as long as you keep them small.

DINING OUT RULES

- Dine out no more than once a week for a single meal.
- Do not dine out until you have stuck to the

acceptable foods list for three weeks. You need time to adjust to this new method of eating at home.

- Go to a quality sit-down restaurant, not a fast food restaurant. If your budget permits, never eat at a chain restaurant that has a television commerical. It usually means the food has been mass produced, and injected with excessive salt, sugar or carbohydrates.
- Go with no more than three other people. With more people, there tends to be too much food on the table and too much temptation.
- Look at the restaurant's menu online ahead of time to make sure it has entrees that match the acceptable foods lists.
- Drink a full glass of water before your meal comes.
- Do not dine out if you have not eaten in more than 4 hours. You are less likely to make smart food choices.
- Stick to water. Do not overload on liquid sugar in wine, mixed drinks, juice, or soda.
- Only dine with individuals who support your lifestyle. Never dine with anyone who says, "Baby, you can have whatever you like."

- Tell the restaurant manager or waiter that you have a health condition that prevents you from eating sugar, dairy, rice, flour or wheat. They will go the extra mile to ensure your food is cooked properly. Many times in restaurants waiters ignore or forget customer's dietary concerns and act annoyed if you just generally mention dietary restrictions. They look at you as just another person trying to lose weight. However, if you throw in a life-or-death health condition, they won't ignore your dietary restrictions.

ACCEPTABLE MENU WORDS

- Baked
- Boiled
- Broiled
- Grilled
- Light
- Marinated
- Poached
- Reduced
- Roasted
- Seasoned
- Steamed

UNACCEPTABLE MENU WORDS

- Au gratin
- Basted
- Béarnaise
- Butter sauce
- Breaded
- Casserole
- Cheesy
- Country-style

- Covered
- Creamed/creamy
- Crispy
- Crunchy
- Escalloped
- Fried/deep-fried
- Giant
- Smothered
- Stroganoff
- Stuffed
- Volcano
- White sauce

SAFE EATING AT ITALIAN RESTAURANTS

EXAMPLES OF WHAT TO ORDER

- Grilled calamari (not fried)
- Salad with balsamic vinegar (no thick and creamy dressings, vinaigrettes, croutons, cheese, or bread)
- Enjoy a roasted or grilled poultry or seafood dish, such as roasted chicken or grilled salmon. Ask for a side of grilled vegetables.

SPECIFIC MENU WORDS TO AVOID

- Breaded
- Parmigiana
- Alfredo
- Scampi
- Crispy/lightly
- Fried/Fritto
- Carbonara

SAFE EATING AT MEXICAN RESTAURANTS

EXAMPLES OF WHAT TO ORDER

- Ceviche
- Tostada salad without the tostada. Ask the waiter not to bring out the tostada at all; otherwise you'll nibble and nibble and end up eating the whole thing.
- Order chicken fajitas without the tortilla, and ask for a side salad.
- Grilled or roasted poultry seafood or poultry with a side salad

SPECIFIC MENU WORDS TO AVOID

- Con queso: topped with cheese
- Refried: fried in lard
- Grande/loaded/supreme. This means that the dish is supersized and served with double servings of all toppings, including cheese, sour cream, and refried beans.
- Deep-fried/crispy
- Chimichanga: a deep-fried burrito

SPECIFIC FOODS TO AVOID

- Tortillas
- Rice

- Margaritas
- Tacos
- Taquitos
- Nachos
- Burritos
- Tamales
- Quesadillas
- Enchiladas
- Flautas
- Chimichangas

SAFE EATING AT CHINESE RESTAURANTS/TAKE OUT

Ask that your meals be made with no corn starch or sugar. Tell the staff that you have diabetes. It works.

SPECIFIC MENU WORDS TO AVOID

- Rice. This includes brown rice, fried rice, and steamed rice.
- General Tso's and sweet-and-sour dishes: cubes of meat coated in cornstarch and eggs, deep-fried, and drenched in a sugar-based syrupy sauce
- Egg rolls and spring rolls: vegetables and meat wrapped in a flour-based dough and deep-fried
- Fried. Stay away from fried seafood, dumplings, and meats.
- Chow. This means that the dish has been stir-fried in loads of unhealthy oils.
- Noodles: lo mein, chow mein, and chow fun

EXAMPLES OF WHAT TO ORDER

- Egg drop soup
- Steamed poultry or seafood with vegetables
- Chicken or shrimp egg foo yung without the gravy
- Mu shu chicken without the wrapper
- Black bean chicken without the rice. Ask that no brown sugar be used.

SAFE EATING AT AMERICAN CASUAL (HOUSTON'S, J. ALEXANDER)

EXAMPLES OF WHAT TO ORDER

- Spinach dip. Ask for celery sticks instead of the tortilla chips.
- Kale salad
- Grilled chicken salad without tortilla strips or croutons. Ask for balsamic vinegar dressing to be on the side.
- Grilled or roasted fish of the day, seafood, or poultry
- Broiled crab cakes with non-starchy vegetables
- Rotisserie or roasted chicken with a side salad or non-starchy vegetable

SAFE EATING AT JAPANESE HIBACHI GRILL OR SUSHI RESTAURANT

SPECIFIC MENU ITEMS TO AVOID

- Fried brown and white rice and noodles
- Tempura (deep-fried), crunch (fried), or dynamite (baked in mayonnaise)
- Rolls made with mayo or cream cheese
- Nigiri. It has rice.

EXAMPLES OF WHAT TO ORDER

- Miso soup, sunomono salad (sliced cucumbers), seaweed salad
- Sashimi (thinly sliced raw fish without rice)
- From the hibachi grill: chicken, fish, shrimp, scallops, other seafood, and vegetables
- Condiments: ginger, wasabi, and low-sodium soy sauce

SAFE EATING IN THE MALL FOOD COURT

If you plan to do a long day of shopping, eat a real meal before leaving the house. Or stop at a sit-down restaurant to have a real meal before you begin your shopping. That way you can burn off your food while at the mall. Healthy food options are seriously limited in the mall food court. I can provide only two options:

- Salads. Do not purchase salads that are pre-soaked in dressings.
- Usually in food courts there is a place where chicken samples on toothpicks are being offered. DO NOT eat the bourbon chicken, but get the blackened chicken with a side of cabbage. The bourbon chicken sauce contains sugar.

SAFE EATING AT YOUR COLLEGE CAFETERIA

Part of my weight loss journey began when I was a college student on a university meal plan. The cafeteria meal plans available at colleges and universities are quite expensive. It is your money—or your parents' money—and you can work with your university's student affairs office or food services director to ensure that meals with foods from the acceptable foods list are prepared for you at every meal. Just as university cafeterias meet the dietary needs of students for religious reasons or medical conditions, they will do the same for an individual needing to lose weight. Provide a copy of the acceptable and unacceptable foods list to your university's food service director. Since your meals will be made especially for you and won't sit under a heat lamp all day, you'll get better quality food. If the administration gives you any resistance, have the person paying for the university meal give him or her a call. In my case it was my mother.

SAFE EATING AT FAMILY ENGAGEMENTS AND IMPORTANT EVENTS

Eat a full meal of acceptable protein and acceptable vegetables before going to an event where you know there will be lots of food. With food already in your belly, you are more likely to make better food choices—and less likely to eat two slices of your grandma's famous sweet potato pie. But if you do go a little overboard, be willing to put in extra work at the gym and skip a dinner out for the current or following week. Don't give up!

SAFE EATING WHEN YOU TRAVEL

Whether you are traveling for work or pleasure, you can still stick to the acceptable foods and possibly save money with these tips.

TIPS FOR EATING WHILE TRAVELING

- Stick to all of the acceptable food rules when eating in restaurants.
- When staying in a hotel room that does not already have a refrigerator, tell the staff at the front desk that you have prescription medication that requires refrigeration. Trust me, they will not ask the name of the medication. However, they are required to provide a refrigerator when you say this. Having a refrigerator in your room will allow you to keep leftover salads from when you dined out earlier or other leftovers that may be safe to eat cold if there is not also a microwave available.
- When booking hotels, there are quality hotels that offer full kitchens with cookware. The hotel's front desk staff will provide you with the location of local grocery stores so that you can purchase and cook your own food. This will save you a lot of money and won't derail your weight loss.

RULES TO FOLLOW EVERY DAY

The rules below should be used to supplement your weight loss efforts. All are actual things I do every day.

Still, you have to eat from the acceptable foods list and implement weekly exercise activities.

Eat cinnamon for breakfast. Eat 1 teaspoon of cinnamon every morning. Have a glass of water on hand to help wash it down. You can also find over-the-counter cinnamon capsules at most drug stores. Cinnamon increases your glucose metabolism and helps burn excess glucose, which is stored as fat in the body. Burning glucose more effectively means losing more weight and will help you feel less hungry. This does not mean that you can eat cinnamon buns and buttery cinnamon-swirl raisin bread. Eating a diet without flour, rice, dairy, grain, and sugar is still the key. There is no way around it.

Eat flaxseed before going to bed to stay regular and prevent constipation. Staying regular *(having regular bowel movements)* keeps you feeling 10 pounds lighter! When you feel lazy or sluggish and then have a good bowel movement, you feel more clear-headed, right? Optimal colon function prevents toxin buildup, which impacts your energy level for exercise. Not having regular bowel movements can make you feel like doing only 20 minutes on the elliptical instead of 45 minutes. To prevent constipation and promote regularity, eat 1 teaspoon of *ground* flaxseed before going to bed. It is an excellent source of dietary fiber. Flaxseed works like little scrubbing bubbles on the intestinal walls, increasing the movement of stools. Plus, this keeps your stomach from looking and feeling bloated. Flaxseed works best when taken with plenty of water! Flaxseed also includes heart-healthy omega-3 fatty acids, which promote glowing skin and strong hair and nails. This is why some lotions, soaps, and shampoos contain flaxseed.

Take care of yourself during your menstrual cycle. Losing blood during our menstrual cycle can cause us to feel too tired to go to the gym and to feel as if we deserve a chocolate free-for-all. The day that I know my period is coming, I take one ferrous sulfate iron pill. My doctor advised this. I encourage you to visit a medical doctor before taking any supplements, even if they are over-the-counter. If your physician gives you a green light for taking iron, never take it with coffee because it blocks absorption. Vitamin C increases iron absorption. If you don't take iron in pill form, eat a handful of raw, dark leafy greens (such as spinach or kale) each day of your period. And add an additional 20 ounces of water to your daily water intake when you're menstruating.

Resist late-night cravings. My best friend grew up poor. She once said, "Whenever I was hungry at night, I just went to sleep." That is my advice to you as well.

THE MEASURE OF YOUR SUCCESS

During my weight loss journey I hardly ever weighed myself. Why? Because I hated it when I exercised like a mad dog and ate super-duper healthy all week and then the scale showed a 3-pound weight gain. I didn't want to hear "*But you're building* muscle" or "*You're a woman, and sometimes you just retain extra water.*" I wanted to see results! Not seeing numbers on the scale go down made me feel depressed, and then I would want to eat a brownie.

As an alternative, I began using clothes as a measure of my success. I would buy a dress, shirt, or pair of jeans two to three sizes too small. At the end of every month, I'd squeeze my way into them until I didn't have to squeeze anymore. During middle school and high school, I wore plus size 26 jeans. When I was able to get into size 16 jeans at the age of 21, I wore them the entire day and did the slide-back, even though there was no music. When an old size 20 dress looked like a potato sack on me, it was a true marker of success. It motivated me to push an extra 15 minutes when exercising and not be tempted by the cookie dough gods. I told myself, "*Who cares about brownies—I don't have to shop at Lane Bryant anymore!*"

FOOD ADDICTION NEVER GOES AWAY

Okay, so consider this one of my rare moments of mentioning "research" again. There are a bunch of research studies that suggest that food addiction produces chemicals in the brain similar to drug addiction. I'm not here to dispute these claims. Combating food addiction takes a lot more than just going to therapy to "identify your reasons for overeating" or having the entire family come together and set goals . . . and sing kumbaya and all eat healthy. Things aren't always that simple. Sometimes you have to take drastic action, too. Some of my advice below may sound over the top. But think about it this way: People put locks on porn, alcohol, and legal and illegal drugs not just so that kids can't get it but, in some cases, adults too. It is time we begin treating food addiction . . . like addiction.

SEVEN SURVIVAL TIPS FOR FOOD ADDICTS

1. Never bring any unacceptable food into your home. I never bring foods containing flour, wheat, rice, grain, dairy, or sugar into my home. Never. Don't think that you can treat yourself to just a little bit of it once in a while. Instead, you

will end up eating the entire box, bag, or tub.

2. Always keep cooked and shredded chicken breasts in sealed plastic bags in your work and home refrigerators. Whenever you feel hungry, eat the chicken breasts and drink water. The protein immediately suppresses your appetite.
3. Eat breakfast within 30 minutes of waking up. You can prepare an omelet at night, place it in a plastic container for storing, and microwave it in the morning. Eating breakfast helps to keep your hunger in check throughout the day. It also prevents you from ordering a pastry at Starbucks.
4. If you live with others who aren't open to healthy eating, buy a separate mini-fridge, deep freezer, and cabinet to keep your acceptable foods. Buy refrigerator and cabinet locks at home improvement stores for the main family refrigerator. The rest of your household can have keys to those locks; you cannot.
5. Say you have a weak moment at the grocery store. You purchased cookies or some other sugary item that was on sale. Now you are at home having a Texas standoff with the sugary item. First, tell those cookies, "These hips aren't big

enough for the both of us." Open the package, spray the food with a household cleaner, and throw it in the trash. I would suggest just throwing it in trash, but some food addicts would dig in the trash for a cookie. A cookie sprayed with a chemical cleaner, not so much.

6. When stressed or feeling like you are about to go after a bag of your favorite food-drug, opt for exercising. A simple walk is fine, but the more strenuous the activity, the more likely it will exorcise that food demon out of you. Exercise produces the brain chemicals known as endorphins, which make you happy!
7. Eat a huge salad or meal of lean protein and vegetables before you leave work. Actually stuff yourself! The overly full feeling will prevent you from wanting to stop at a fast food joint on the way home. Or making unhealthy choices if stopping at the grocery store before heading home from the office. Also, if you feel overly full from healthy food, you are less likely to raid the fridge as soon as you walk in the door from work.

SAYING NO TO FOOD PUSHERS

"Aww, go on and treat yourself a little." Family, especially older relatives like grandmothers and great aunts, are the Nino Browns of food pushing—especially during the holidays and family events. Some older people tend to not understand the concept of dieting since they come from a time when having lots of food was a good thing. Giving in to one biscuit or a slice of pound cake can cause you to feel like you have messed up completely, so you should just give up and have another biscuit or slice of cake. Some would say that moderation is the answer here, but it is not. Trust me, once you get a taste of food you have not had in a long time, you will want and eat more and more of it.

The tactful way to handle a food pusher is to tell them one of two things: (1) "I am allergic." Even if it is someone who has known you all your life, some people actually develop various food allergies later in life (myself included.); or (2) "I can't eat that because of a medication I am taking."

HERE ARE THREE PUSHES AND HOW TO HANDLE THEM

1. "You know this is my specialty, try it!"

- Your response: "I will in just a sec, let me go wash my hands." Or if it is a dessert they are offering say, "Let me eat some real food first." If they ask you later if you tried it, respond, "Yep, you really put your foot in it."
- Why it works: If the person made a specialty, it is likely a well-attended event where the person will move on to pushing the dish on other people and forget about you.

2. "Girl, have some. You know you don't need to lose no weight! You need to put some meat on your bones!"
   - Your response: "Yes, I do. I am not trying to end up like {insert family member name} with diabetes or heart problems."
   - Why it works: Bringing up diabetes or heart disease will shut anyone up. Also, the personal touch of how these diseases may have affected a family member helps as well.

3. "Have another drink." Or "Let's get another round."
   - Your response: "No, I can't. I'm driving."
   - Why it works: Family or true friends typically won't argue with your preference to drive home

sober. If they do, you probably should get a new drinking buddy. Also, you can get out of the situation by saying you have an early morning meeting at work or a doctor's appointment or that you have to take someone to one. Bring up kids, too—it works like a charm!

BE S.M.A.R.T. ABOUT YOUR GOALS

My motivation to maintain my weight loss lies in refusing to allow myself to be part of the negative health statistics I hear on the news pertaining to African-Americans about such things as diabetes, hypertension, and heart disease. There must be a sturdy bridge between motivation and setting goals. My motivation not to gain weight led me to set smaller goals. This included preparing my meals for the week on Sunday night or trying a new fitness activity once a month. Individual motivations to lose weight may be different. Ideally, it should be to improve your overall health and live a longer life. For most it is, but beneath this motivation lie other superficial reasons for wanting to lose weight. Whatever your motives, setting goals too high will discourage you, while goals set too low will leave you feeling "empty" when you are done. I encourage you to set straightforward goals for weight loss using the S.M.A.R.T principles:

S – Specific
M – Measurable
A – Attainable
R – Realistic
T – Time sensitive

Specific. If you make your goals as specific as possible, it is more likely they will be accomplished. Instead of merely saying "I need to lose some weight and get in shape," be specific. For example:

- I want to lose 30 pounds.
- I want to go down two dress sizes.

Measurable. It is important to have a way to measure your progress, both in the short term and in the long term. This also helps to keep you motivated. For example:

- I will be able to walk a mile and a half instead of just a mile at the end of the month. (Short term)
- I want to lose 100 pounds by the end of the year. (Long term)

Attainable. This means making sure that your goals match your current lifestyle, work schedule, and family obligations. For example:

- I will walk in the evening after dinner.
- I will do Zumba on Tuesdays and Thursdays when my husband gets off of work early.

Realistic. If you haven't exercised in years, don't set yourself up for failure by planning to run 4 miles in one day, especially if you were never a runner. Also, planning to be the size of a certain celebrity within two months may not be the most manageable, either. To be realistic, your goals must ones that you are *willing* and *able* to accomplish. Your goals are probably realistic if you truly *believe* that they can be accomplished. For example:

- I want to be able to zip my pre-pregnancy jeans.
- I will use the elliptical for 30 minutes for five days a week.

Time sensitive. Set a time frame for when you want to fully accomplish your weight loss goals. Picking a deadline for shedding weight will give you a sense of urgency and accountability. It always helped me to connect my motivation to an important event.

- I want to lose 20 pounds before my brother's wedding.
- I want to lose all my weight before our family reunion next year.

MOTIVATION AND WAYS TO REWARD YOURSELF

Motivation reinforces the self-discipline needed to overcome food temptations and discouragement. The best way to keep your motivation high is to reward yourself when you reach short-term goals throughout your journey. This could be each time you lose 5 or 10 pounds, if you do choose to weigh yourself. Or when you go from doing 20 to 40 minutes on the elliptical. Or when your doctor tells you your blood pressure is lower. Celebrate as your budget, schedule, and interests allow.

Identify non-food rewards for your successes. Going out to celebrate at an all-you-can-eat buffet after you have lost 20 pounds compromises your weight loss plans and, quite frankly, doesn't make any sense. Instead, consider the following ideas:

Treat yourself. Splurge on a weekend getaway, a spa day, fitness classes, a boudoir photo shoot, going shopping, manicures, pedicures, or hair services rather than food. (Keep an eye on discount or coupon websites to help you keep the cost manageable.) These are all things that will make you feel good inside and out. In particular, the photo shoot may help you really see how much weight you have lost. Weird, but for me, I could never see my weight loss changes in the mirror—only in photos.

Help others. Volunteer on weekends or once a month for a cause that is important to you. Tutor at an inner-city school, edit résumés at a domestic violence shelter, or serve meals at homeless shelter. Volunteering at these types of places makes you feel good and makes all of the problems that led you to food seem so minor.

Visit friends or family. They tend to show the most excitement and encouragement about your weight loss efforts. Expect comments such as "Oh my gosh, you look so good" and "I am so proud of you!" You are already well aware of the friends and family members who are haters, so stay away from them.

Share your progress. Post before and after photos on Facebook or an online health forum where you are a member. Friends and complete strangers online will provide you with motivation and tips. And we all have a little bit of vanity in us.

CHAPTER 5

EXERCISE: LOSING WEIGHT TAKES WORK

CAROLINE'S COMMANDMENT #9

Exercise! The drug everyone can afford!

IN THE WORDS of the illustrious Prince, "You don't have to be rich"—to exercise. When I began my weight loss journey as a broke college student, my primary form of exercise was walking to and from my summer internship instead of catching the bus. This was free.

YOU DON'T HAVE TO BE RICH

Of course, walking alone is not always enough. I have learned that in life you don't have to be rich, but you do have to be a hustler. Here are affordable recommendations on workout options that have been helpful to me:

LivingSocial/Groupon/Yelp. All of these websites offer discounted coupons or vouchers for gym memberships, various fitness classes, personal training, and fitness boot camps. This allows you to sample different activities and perhaps identify a physical activity you will enjoy over the long term.

Local YMCA. The first gym I joined was a local YMCA, which offered a discounted membership that was based on my zero-income as a student. In addition to full use of exercise machines and weights, I enjoyed fitness classes like step aerobics and had open access to the racquetball courts.

Local community center and religious centers. Many have fitness classes or gym facilities open to the public.

Guest passes at gyms. Depending on your location, there might be a gym on every corner. When I was home in downtown Washington, D.C., I got a three- to five-day guest pass every week at various gyms. For the two months that I was in the city, I worked out and didn't pay a single dime.

Free YouTube fitness videos. There are great workout videos on YouTube created by everyday people. You can get your workout on right in front of your laptop for free!

Bicycling. I ride my bicycle almost everywhere I go—to work, bookstores, and even sometimes to the grocery store. I've done this since I was in college. Bicycles are a great way to improve knee strength for those with knee problems. If you haven't ridden a bike in years, just get on one. It really is something you never forget how to do.

Computer/video game software. Almost video game consoles now offer dance and exercise videos for purchase. If you or your kids already have a console, you can make exercise a family activity.

Walking outdoors. I want to revisit this, even though I mentioned it in the introduction. You may not think you can fit walking into your day, but I bet you can. Walk to work or to meet friends instead of taking the bus, subway, or your car. If you don't think you can do that every day, try it for just one day each week. Walk your kids to school or to their friends' places—you'll be helping yourself and teaching them good habits at the same time. Take the stairs instead of the elevator. In your office building, use a restroom on a different floor. You may not think walking does enough. But it can do a lot! My walk to and from work covered 4 miles of very hilly areas. Within two months of walking five days a week and eating acceptable foods, I lost 30 pounds.

WALKING TIPS

- **Wear a weighted vest.** If you live in an area of the country, like the Midwest, where the terrain is flat, purchase a women's weighted vest to wear during your walks. Weighted vests evenly distribute the weight throughout your body unlike ankle or arm weights, which can cause unhealthy muscle strain. Weighted vests can be purchased in sporting good stores or online. Look for a 20-pound vest that will allow you to add and remove weight. I began walking with about 8 pounds of weight and then worked my way up to using the entire 20 pounds.
- **Buy quality running shoes.** Be sure to invest in good athletic sneakers for all of your exercise activities to prevent injury. Don't pick an exercise shoe just because you find it cute and feminine.

No matter what fitness activity you plan to engage in, visit a specialty athletic or running shoe store. These stores have many methods to assess your foot type and the type of foot support you need.

- **Be safe when walking outdoors.** Walk with at least one other person. That's the best way to be safe, but I enjoyed the time to myself walking alone. To stay safe when you're alone, keep the volume of your headphone music low so that you can hear what is going on around you. Always wear reflective gear when walking in the early morning hours or evening. Before heading out, be sure that someone knows your exact walking route and the times you usually head out and return from your walks.
- **Track your progress with your smartphone.** There are many applications that you can download to your smartphone to help you keep track of your daily distance, speed, and route. This provides tools for measuring your progress and can help you to increase both speed and distance day by day. Most of these applications also allow you to share your hard work on your Facebook page or through Twitter. People will commend you, but you may also inspire others as well.

MORE EXERCISE IDEAS

It wouldn't be fair for me to say that one type of exercise helps you burn more calories than another. Each person's body responds differently to various forms of exercise. Also, not everyone likes the same fitness activities. Engaging in a physical activity that you find enjoyable is key—otherwise you won't stick with it.

Below I include the various fitness activities that helped me keep the pounds down and that were quite enjoyable. Keep in mind that to accelerate weight loss, you have to work your way up to 45 minutes of physical activity five to six days a week. While studies suggest that 20 minutes of brisk walking on flat terrain in your neighborhood is good for overall heart health, it won't be enough for weight loss.

Step aerobics. In the early stages of my journey I took a step aerobics class three times a week at a local community center. Once I got my coordination together, I sweated like crazy and actually enjoyed it.

Elliptical fitness trainer. This cardio machine really helped me shed my last chunk of weight. Also, this machine is great for those who have knee or joint issues. For maximum results, don't hold on to the rails and go backward. This forces you to engage your abs for balance, and the backward motion will make your booty look great!

Water aerobics. Don't worry about your hair getting wet. Most of the movements are done above water. And, no, water aerobics is not just for seniors. You really have to put in a lot of force to work your body against the water.

Boot camp. I took part in indoor and outdoor boot camps. From climbing stairs to completing obstacle courses—I enjoyed it all. Also, it brought out a bit of a competitive streak in me to always want to work harder and go faster than the other people around me. The work you do in boot camps will constantly surprise your body, which is great for weight loss.

Build a home gym. After years of gym memberships, getting up in the cold to go to the gym and then having to wait in line to use a treadmill, I built a home gym. I researched consumer websites and invested in a quality treadmill, elliptical, stationary bike, and free weights. I am in love. I can exercise whenever I want, in my drawers, and blare my dirty-South hip-hop as loud as I please. Yeeeeeeeeeeah!

Cardio boxing. This is therapy in the form of boxing gloves. Always feel free to pretend the punching bag is an ex-boyfriend or your boss. Also, cardio boxing involves nonstop movement; therefore, your heart rate stays up, causing extra calories and fat in all parts of the body to burn away.

Dance around your house like a video girl. On nights when I feel sluggish from a heavy dinner or I need to motivate myself to begin my workout, this is what I do. I would recommend that you try anything by Beyoncé or from what is known as "crunk" hip-hop. But don't make this your only workout method!

Crossfit. If you have tried every exercise on the block and still can't lose weight, give Crossfit a try. It is a high intensity and strength training workout. You will feel like Shera in every class. Google "Crossfit" for more information and classes in your town.

TIPS ON FINDING A PERSONAL TRAINER

If you do decide to join a gym, I encourage working with a personal trainer to get acquainted with a routine:

- Be sure that your prospective trainer has completed a personal training certification program from an NCAA-accredited organization: The American College of Sports Medicine, National Strength and Conditioning Association, American Council on Exercise, and National

Academy of Sports Medicine are all respected within the industry. In addition to checking for these certifications, ask if the trainer has any supplemental education in the field. If possible, find a trainer with a degree in an exercise science, kinesiology, or a physical education program. If weight loss or toning is your goal, ask for before and after pictures of previous clients. Treat prospective personal trainers like a job candidate: Ask for their resúme. Remember your body is your resúme.

- Take advantage of the free one-on-one consultation (which includes discussion of fitness goals and a light to moderate personal training session) that the trainer should offer. You want to make sure you get along—since you will work with this person closely—and that you like the workout styles.
- Ask what types of activities you will be doing in the real sessions. For weight loss the body needs variation and innovation! Find a trainer who will mix up workouts and keep them fun and creative.
- Visit the facility at the hours you plan to train! Is it a comfortable place for you at that time? Don't forget to check out the bathrooms.

LOOKING GOOD WHILE YOU'RE SWEATING

A friend once said that she doesn't like to exercise unless she has cute workout clothes. She is not alone, of course. And the fitness clothing industry has taken note. I've seen workout pants in designer sportswear stores for 40 to 60 bucks. I just think that's way too much to pay for clothes used for sweating. Here's a list of my favorite stores to find bargain workout gear:

DISCOUNT STORES

I know, I know: Clothes and sizes in these stores are never organized. The aisles are really small. Try to go at an unpopular time of day, when the rest of the world is at work. Most of the stuff will be freshly stocked. New arrivals tend to come in Tuesday through Thursday.

Ross. This is my favorite! Whether on Ross's regular or clearance racks, I've found Nike, Reebok, and no-name sports bras and yoga pants for 3 to 7 bucks.

Walmart. Walmart's stuff, of course, is the cheapest on the block. Walmart also carries fitness clothes in plus sizes. However, in terms of colors and cool designs, Walmart is a little limited.

Old Navy. You can find reasonably priced fitness

clothes primarily on the clearance racks, some on the regular racks.

Target. Target has lots of fitness clothes with bright and tropical colors. Many of their fitness items have built-in bra and belly support. Also, while at Target you can pick up toilet paper, dish detergent, and anything else you may need around the house!

TJ Maxx/Marshall's (owned by the same company). They have great pieces, but TJ Maxx's and Marshall's prices have gone up a little. Here and there I've found high-quality fitness gear for good prices, but not lately. Check the prices before you buy.

EXERCISE AND KEEPING YOUR HAIR CLEAN

Yes, I have heard about black women not exercising because of hair maintenance issues. We all have various hair textures and types that respond differently to sweat, so I am unable to make specific styling recommendations for everyone. However, I can provide advice on keeping your scalp clean and not smelling like death. Although most black women don't have the option of shampooing their hair after every workout, it is still very important to cleanse sweat and bacteria from the scalp after exercise.

TIPS ON KEEPING YOUR HAIR FRESH

Whether you have braids, a weave, or a natural 'do, these tips can help you keep your hair fresh in between washes.

- In a clean, resealable plastic bottle, combine 8 ounces of witch hazel, 8 ounces of spring water, and about 10 drops of pure tea tree oil. Keep this concoction stored in your refrigerator. It will help to soothe the scalp after your workouts.
- Make one braid, preferably a French braid, and then clip the braid up.
- Tie a 100 percent silk (not polyester-blend) scarf around your edges. *I created homemade silk scarves by cutting pieces from old clothing.*
- After your workout, loosen the braid. Using a white washcloth or towel, work through your hair, parting it in rows, soaking up as much sweat as possible out of the hair.
- Dampen a clean white washcloth with the scalp-soothing mixture. Following the same parting routine, rub the washcloth through your hair.
- Give your hair a chance to breathe and dry a little before restyling.

CHAPTER 6

THE HIGHS AND LOWS OF RECOVERY

CAROLINE'S COMMANDMENT #10

Happy 30th birthday!
It is also your metabolism's
retirement party!

SINCE I ENTERED my 30s, my metabolism has already considering planning her retirement party, and all of my she-gets-it-from-her-mama genetics have begun to kick in. All my life people have told me that my face looks like my mother's, but once I hit age 30, my body started to want to look like my mother's and grandmother's bodies in the hips, waist, butt, and thighs. (The breasts not so much.) People often ask, "How long do you eat only the acceptable foods? Can you sneak some sweets in here and there?" Before the age of 30 I would have likely said, "Sure, as long as you remember to exercise a little extra during your next workout." These days, that does not fly. If I eat a cupcake or even something made of whole grain, it sticks to these hips like an unwanted houseguest, no matter how much of a maniac workout I do. What always works and gets me back on track is eating from the acceptable foods list. I am not saying my method is the be-all and end-all, but 10 years of experience has taught me that this is the method of healthy eating that works best for *my* body. If you are able to sneak in breads, rice, sweet potatoes, or an occasional slice of chocolate cake throughout your weight loss journey and still see week-to-week weight loss results, hallelujah, and I am totally jealous.

In addition to getting older, individuals can experience plateaus or stalls in their weight loss for a number of medical and lifestyle reasons. For clarity, a weight-loss stall or plateau occurs when you no longer lose weight despite continuing with your exercise and healthy eating habits. This can be very frustrating. You should always visit your doctor first—to determine possible causes of weight-loss stalls and plateaus.

WEIGHT-LOSS STALLS AND PLATEAUS

Outside of hitting the big 3-0, here are some other reasons behind weight-loss stalls and plateaus that I experienced firsthand:

Vitamin D deficiency. Vitamin D helps our brains control hunger and cravings. Additionally, vitamin D boosts levels of serotonin, which is a brain chemical that keeps us in a happy mood. Most importantly, vitamin D helps the body absorb calcium. When the body doesn't absorb calcium, its process of metabolizing fat slows down. Only a medical doctor can determine if you are vitamin D or iron deficient. If you are indeed deficient in vitamin D, food and over-the-counter supplements will not be effective by themselves. You need prescription-strength help that you can't get online. You need to see a medical doctor, preferably an endocrinologist.

Iron deficiency. Iron provides the body's cells with the oxygen they need to function. Without enough iron you'll feel tired and perhaps too lazy to workout. Since exercise is essential for weight loss, you need iron! Note: I have been tagged as "iron deficient" since I was a baby.

Not drinking enough water. Water runs the transportation system that gets fat of your body. Make sure you are drinking half your body weight in ounces of water each day. Do not count your coffee or tea intake as water.

Hidden carbohydrates and sugar. Watch out for hidden wheat, flour, sugar, and dairy in soups, salad dressings, and other condiments and even some meat used in salad bars and restaurants.

Eating too little. Terms like portion control and reducing calorie intake have been drilled into our head so much that they are hard habits to break. Remember to eat a source of lean protein and non-starchy vegetables every 2 to 3 hours. Going without food for 4 or 5 hours will cause the body to slow down your metabolism and conserve existing fat, not burn it.

Not including weight-resistance training in your exercise regimen. Bouncing around on the treadmill and elliptical for cardiovascular exercise won't burn fat alone. You must include some form of weight training at least three times a week to boost your metabolism. Muscle burns fat, and it continues to burn fat even as we sit at our desk or sleep.

Food allergies. Food allergies and intolerances can

be difficult to identify and may arise even if you never had the allergy before or as a child. I developed most of my food allergies after hitting puberty and as an adult. Food allergies can trigger weight gain, fluid retention, and constipation and diarrhea. To identify possible food allergies, visit an allergist.

Medications. Medications such as steroids, oral contraceptives, insulin, oral diabetic medications and psychotropic drugs such as antidepressants can decrease fat burning and in some cases increase fat storage. However, do NOT by any means stop use of these medications without a doctor's supervision.

You're not eating enough fat. To lose fat, the body actually needs healthy fats. Increase your intake of fish rich in omega-3 fats such as salmon, which is my personal favorite. Liquid omega-3 oil or cod liver oil that is refrigerated in health food stores is also a good option. Again the unrefrigerated fish oil capsules in drugstores and the grocery store are not as potent. One tablespoon of fish oil a day will go a long way.

Too much caffeine. Caffeine can cause a drop in blood sugar levels, which leads to sugar cravings and binge eating. Drinking caffeine can possibly cause the overproduction of insulin and insulin resistance. Too much insulin in your system can stall weight loss and even cause weight gain. For some, caffeine may feel like an appetite suppressant at first, but eventually the body crashes and craves more caffeine and sometimes sugary food.

You reward yourself with food. People often allow themselves to have things like dessert or extra food because they went to the gym earlier or had a salad for lunch. These antics without a doubt will cause weight gain and perhaps cause you to eat more because of the disappointment of not being able to buckle your jeans. Focus on how hard you have been exercising and the number of sweaty bad hair days you have had to endure, and then remind yourself that the dessert or other unacceptable item you are planning to reward yourself with isn't even worth it.

Get plenty of sleep. When the body doesn't get enough sleep, it goes into survival mode, and your metabolism will move at a snail-like pace. When you are sleep deprived, not only does your body hold on tightly to existing fat, but it will also feel as if it needs excessive food (*usually unhealthy food*) to support the lack of sleep. This is why when you're sleepy in the middle of the day, you reach for doughnuts or a sugary coffee drink. To lose weight, get 8 hours of sleep each night. If your exercise duration is 60 minutes or more, get 10 hours of sleep for full recovery. Instead of chatting with a coworker or checking Facebook during your lunch break, take a nap in an empty office conference room.

If you find that you are still experiencing a weight-loss stall or plateau despite resolving all of the other possible stall/plateau reasons, you may want to try becoming a pescatarian, which means only eating seafood as a source of lean protein and sticking to the rest of the acceptable food rules. Seafood is not cheap, but buying frozen seafood won't kill your pocketbook as much.

AFTER THE STORM: PLASTIC SURGERY

As a result of my weight loss I was left with masses of skin that hung like curtains from my belly and beneath my arms. The fact that my stomach was now bigger than my breasts bothered me the most. People often commented that my belly looked like the stomach of a woman that had had five kids, even though I have never had children.

I know of others who were successful at losing more than 100 pounds with no issues with sagging skin. Their skin bounced back. However, for many, myself included, there was no amount of exercise or strength training that would get rid of my post-weight-loss flab.

In December 2007, I chose to have an abdominoplasty (tummy tuck) and liposuction on my arms to remove the excess skin. I thought that the skin weighed more, but the doctor said it was around a pound and half worth of skin that he removed.

Over the last few years I maintained a flat belly with more intensive cardiovascular exercise. You must engage in serious shirt-soaking SWEAT, meaning cardio, to burn fat around the belly. A million crunches and Pilates won't do it alone. I am 50/50 concerning whether I would have plastic surgery again, maybe on my thighs. My hesitancy is because the surgery was the worst—let me say it again, the worst—pain of my life. Maybe I am just a sucker. After the surgery it hurt when I laughed, it hurt when I breathed, it hurt when I walked, it hurt when I ate . . . and for some reason I couldn't urinate after surgery unless I splashed ice cold water on my vajayjay with a water bottle and shocked it to pee. My doctor said it was normal and happens to some women after C-sections. Go figure.

TIPS ON FINDING A PLASTIC SURGEON

With all of the recent plastic surgery horror stories that have hit the news, I also wanted to include some basic tips in identifying a good plastic surgeon.

- **Ask a friend or relative.** More than likely a family member, family friend, or someone at your hairdresser or fitness class has also had plastic surgery or knows of someone who did. This person can provide you with contact information for a prospective surgeon and share their experience in terms of the doctor's bedside manner and skill, the surgery process, and recovery.
- **Look for a plastic surgeon that is certified by the American Board of Plastic Surgeons and a member of the American Society of Plastic Surgeons.** Contact these associations directly with the name and office location of your prospective plastic surgeon to verify. Do not accept any certificates or diplomas on the plastic surgeon's walls as proof of certification. Faux degrees and certifications can be created online.
- **Check the surgeon's records.** Malpractice rulings against doctors are typically public information. Ask the surgeon directly, and search public court records. Google can be a powerful thing.
- **Experience counts.** The plastic surgeon you choose should have 10 or more years of experience not just as a doctor but doing the specific procedure you are requesting. In general, the

more experience the physician has in performing a certain procedure, the better the results and recovery.

- **Ask if the surgeon has hospital privileges.** Many plastic surgeons operate out of outpatient clinics, but ask if the surgeon has hospital privileges because hospitals tend to do thorough background checks. Also, if a medical emergency occurs during your operation in the outpatient clinic, it is better for the performing doctor to have hospital privileges with a nearby emergency room. If the prospective plastic surgeon does not have hospital privileges, consider it a red flag.
- **If your plastic surgeon works out of an outpatient clinic, make sure it is an accredited facility.** Accredited means the facility has been inspected by an accrediting organization or local health department and meets strict standards designed to protect patients. If the facility is not accredited, it may not be fully prepared to handle an emergency.
- **Does your surgeon teach?** If the plastic surgeon has an academic appointment at a university or a hospital teaching other doctors how to perform plastic surgery, consider that a very good

thing. Now, if the prospective surgeon suggests that academic appointments are not important, look for another surgeon.

- **Ask for photos.** When having a consultation with a potential plastic surgeon, ask to see before and after photos of patients that had the procedure you are considering. Ask if there are any patients willing to let you contact them about their experiences. If the doctor is hesitant to show pictures, does not have many pictures, or acts strange when you ask to contact previous patients, go elsewhere.
- **Communication.** During the consultation with the plastic surgeon, be sure that the doctor is patient and friendly and thoroughly answers all your questions regarding possible risks, side effects, and recovery.

TEN YEARS AND COUNTING! LOVING LIFE MORE THAN FOOD!

ANYONE WHO CALLS bull on my method to healthy eating must first realize that I am the healthy lab rat in my own experiment: I am the living proof. Some may say that my healthy eating method may not work because it is too much of a departure from "normal" eating habits, too difficult in today's world where bread, pasta, and other wheat products are on every corner, and that it is even more unrealistic because people have been trained to crave sweet. Well, I say it is even more difficult to live in a world where you are ashamed to go to your kid's school because of how you look, you can barely make it up a flight of stairs in your mid-20s, people stare at you when you eat in public, you are unable to buckle your seatbelt, or your weight has prevented you from ever having a romantic relationship. These are all things I have experienced or that people close to me have. Individuals have to decide what is more important to them, having their cake and eating it too, or truly being able to live life to the fullest. As far as I know, we get only one.

Losing weight has lifted the pause button from my enjoying simple things in life. I am able to race my five nephews (and *almost* win). When shopping, I buy clothes that make me feel like a woman. I can look at my body and see hips, breasts, and curves that during puberty were hidden beneath mounds of fat on my body. Heck, it also helps that since I lost weight I can finally find clothes in my size on the sale racks when shopping. When riding roller coasters, the safety bar can now go down over my stomach—although I realized I wasn't really missing much because roller coasters scare the crap out of me.

Whether at work, at school, or walking down the street, I am more confident in all that I do, yet the bumpy path it took to get here keeps me humble. In addition to becoming physically stronger, my weight loss journey also strengthened me emotionally. Don't get me wrong. Losing 150 pounds has not made me immune to life's stresses. Tough situations still arise with family, work, friendships, and relationships. When problems arise, there are still times when I want to lock myself away from the world with my old drug buddies Ben and Jerry (ice cream). But instead of running to get a spoon, I pause and remind myself that all tough situations are temporary. Although I have a good grasp on managing stress, I am always open to returning to therapy if needed. But even better than any therapist's couch is resting my head on my biological father's Santa-like belly. More than losing 150 pounds, our renewed relationship is truly life's greatest reward. If I am having a rough day, I visit him at his auto shop. We may not even discuss whatever has made my day rough. But lying on his belly and listening to his stories of growing up as a boy in Guyana and impersonating my grandmother Caroline's voice as she gave him chores or taught him to cook makes me forget why I may have been having a rough day in the first place. Nothing else seems to matter. I wish that my dad could have been more of a constant figure in my early life, but, as my mom says, there is no use in crying over spilled milk. What I have learned is that "Life is like a bicycle: To keep your balance you have to keep moving forward." Part of keeping my forward momentum and finding my balance is literally through exercise.

Exercise has become both an antidepressant and an appetite suppressant. Not sure what it is; I just know that the more I exercise, the less I think about and want chocolate chip cookie dough, bacon, and pasta. When I don't exercise or miss workouts, I have a funky attitude and come close to pressing E7 on the office vending machine for a glazed honey bun. Exercise for me has in essence become what methadone is to heroin addicts. It has helped to wean me off unhealthy food choices—particularly sugar. My motto has become, "I eat every day, so I exercise every day." I don't work out every day because I love it: I work out because there is a part of me that feels I have to.

The recipe of my family, especially reuniting with my daddy, plus disciplined eating and consistent exercise has taken my passion for food from a dirty love affair to a committed relationship of self-control.

RESOURCES FOR FOOD ADDICTION

AS I MENTIONED earlier in the book, please talk to your primary care doctor and ob/gyn, who can refer you to a combination of other doctors, psychotherapists, and nutritionists who specialize in battling food addiction. Many licensed health and wellness professionals who treat food addiction can be found through a quick Google search. One way to determine if they are legitimate medical professionals is whether your insurance company will actually cover their treatment costs. Still, there are many qualified medical professionals who don't take insurance and see only self-pay patients. You have to consider what best meets your needs and budget. However, you should consider your mental health as priceless. Below, I have included other information for no-cost support groups:

ANOREXICS AND BULIMICS ANONYMOUS

- *www.aba12steps.org*

"ABA uses the Twelve-Step Program adapted from Alcoholics Anonymous to address the mental, emotional, and spiritual components of the disorders of anorexia and bulimia. Many people who identify compulsive overeating as the primary component of their eating disorder have been able to relate to our program and have found recovery through it. They are welcome to participate in our Fellowship."

FOOD ADDICTS IN RECOVERY ANONYMOUS

- *www.foodaddicts.org*

"Food Addicts in Recovery Anonymous is an international fellowship of men and women who have experienced difficulties in life as a result of the way we eat. Participants joined FA either because they could not control our eating or because they were obsessed with food."

OVEREATERS ANONYMOUS

- *www.oa.org*

"Overeaters Anonymous offers a program of recovery from compulsive eating using the Twelve Steps and Twelve Traditions of OA. Worldwide meetings and other tools provide a fellowship of experience, strength and hope where members respect one another's anonymity. OA charges no dues or fees; it is self-supporting through member contributions. OA is not just about weight loss, weight gain or maintenance, or obesity or diets. It addresses physical, emotional and spiritual well-being. It is not a religious organization and does not promote any particular diet."